FALLING IN LOVE
WITH WHERE YOU ARE

A Year of Prose and Poetry
On Radically Opening Up
To the Pain and Joy of Life

Jeff Foster

NON-DUALITY PRESS

FALLING IN LOVE WITH WHERE YOU ARE
First English edition published December 2013 by NON-DUALITY PRESS

Cover design from an idea by Nic Higham. Layout by John Gustard.
Author portrait (back cover) by Liya Matiosova: www.matiosova.book.fr

ISBN:978-1-908664-39-6

NON-DUALITY PRESS | PO Box 2228 | Salisbury | SP2 2GZ
United Kingdom

For Sherie,
forever in my heart.

I will not forget you.

I have held you in the palm of my hand.

– Isaiah 49: 15-16

The bad news is you're falling through the air,

nothing to hang on to, no parachute.

The good news is there's no ground.

– Chögyam Trungpa Rinpoche

In your hands you hold the potential for a total re-ordering of your life as you know it.

In my work in the publishing industry over the last 20+ years, I've had the rare opportunity to get to know and work with hundreds of the world's most respected and realised spiritual teachers, psychologists, psychotherapists, neuroscientists and artists. From time to time, a new voice comes onto the scene – unfortunately for all of us not often enough – with something that is utterly *alive*, emerging out of the unknown, opening a portal into the ever deepening mysteries of love. Jeff Foster is one of these voices.

Over the last few years, I have continued to be inspired by Jeff, both as a writer and someone who cares deeply about the lives of those around him. I have witnessed Jeff sitting with those in deep despair, profound fear and raging anxiety – even on the brink of suicide – struggling with what it really means to be a human being. I have also seen Jeff meet the most devoted spiritual seekers, creating a home for them to come to rest, finally, from the weariness that seeking spiritual enlightenment so often brings. In each of these meetings – through his words, through his silence, and through his loving attunement – Jeff shares the gift of presence, wisdom, clarity and kindness, never giving up on the preciousness and potential of each and every unique person, and of the very human journey itself.

As so many have observed over the last few decades, while the world's great nondual spiritual teachings offer a vision of crystal clarity into the true nature of the eternal Self beyond that which comes and goes, these very same traditions can become stale, worn out, second-hand, and just, well, inhuman. We sometimes forget that the essence of spirituality is a cosmic *embrace* of the relative, the dual, the very messy, sticky, gooey nature of human life. The light we seek is not 'elsewhere', but already shining through the appearance of a separate self, pouring out of our intimate relationships and illuminating our most disturbing feelings and emotions. As Jeff reveals so clearly and provocatively, light is alive even in the darkness.

One of the most important contributions Jeff makes to the spiritual conversation is his uncompromising demand that we honour our humanity and that we take the risk of seeing how sacred "ordinary life" really is. I whole-heartedly recommend this lovely new book of poetry and prose, and sincerely hope that through Jeff's words – and through the space between them – you come to see the magnificence that you are, and begin to consider the real possibility that you've never actually left Home.

Matt Licata, Ph.D. (alovinghealingspace.blogspot.com)
Boulder, Colorado
October 2013

AUTHOR'S NOTE

Who knows who wrote that song of summer

the blackbirds sing at dusk? This is a song of colour,

where sands sing in crimson, red and rust,

then climb into bed and turn to dust....

– Kate Bush, Sunset

Why do I write books about the wordless essence of life? Why do I try to say the unsayable?

Perhaps 'why' is the wrong question. It seems that the deeper the inner silence, the more naturally and effortlessly the words flow, finally liberated from their shackles, set free from the prison of conformity and correctness and the need to be liked or even heard. Out of purest stillness, this delicious music erupts, these creative and playful notes of myself, vibrant expressions of that pre-verbal silence at the core of everything, inviting you to intimacy with your present moment, here and now. My words are your words are the words of life itself, ever offering themselves in remembrance of that which is never gone and is endlessly shining.

I do not write nor speak by myself, for myself, nor am I myself written or spoken, I can only remain radically open to the unexpected eruption of words. I am a house, ready for the children who call me *Home* to come running back from school, their cheeks rosy and stuffed full of chocolate and expectation, and ready to let them go, as they finally leave for destinations and adventures unknown.

It's like asking the blackbirds why they sing in summer.

Friend, if you are experiencing stress, sorrow, physical or emotional pain in your life right now, it doesn't mean that your life is going wrong, that you are broken and sinful, that you have failed as a human or spiritual being, or that you are far from awakening. *You may just be healing in your own original and unexpected way.* Sometimes we need to feel worse for a while. Sometimes the old structures, things that we once defined and identified as 'me', need to crumble. Sometimes we need to be brought to our knees before we can stand again. Sometimes illusions need to die. Sometimes our sacred plans and hopes, our schemes and dreams of "how things were going to turn out", need to burn to ashes on the ruthless yet ultimately compassionate bonfire of the present moment.

As we open up to life and love and healing, as we awaken from our dream of separateness, we meet not just the bliss of existence, but also its pain; not only the ecstasy of life, but its agony too. Awakening doesn't always feel good or comforting or blissful or 'spiritual', for we are inevitably forced to confront our deepest fears and darkest shadows – those parts of ourselves that we have cut-off, denied, repressed, numbed ourselves to all these years, and the meeting can get messy to say the least.

But eventually we come to trust the process of no process at all. We learn to see even our deepest sorrow as an intelligent movement *of* life, not a threat *to* life. We remember that we are vast enough to hold all of it – the good and the bad, the pain and the pleasure, the light and the dark, the agony and the ecstasy. We are not nearly as limited as we once imagined. We are life itself.

Falling In Love With Where You Are offers a simple but radical invitation: *Stop waiting for the world to make you happy.* Stop making your inner joy dependent on external things – objects, people, circumstances, experiences, events – that are out of your direct control right now. Stop playing the happiness lottery. Give yourself a break from seeking and discover the natural happiness that you are and have always been, the in-built contentment that doesn't depend on life's ever-changing 'content'.

The prose and poetry in this book, harvested from two years' worth of journal entries and Facebook posts, is designed to guide, challenge, encourage and perhaps inspire you on your lonely, painful, ecstatic, crazy, exhausting, blissful and confusing pathless journey to the Home that you never, ever abandoned: the present moment.

Read the following pages slowly, mindfully. Spend twelve months soaking everything in, meditating on the words as the seasons change within and around you. Or, whenever the mood takes you, allow the book to fall open at a random page. Let the words in this book live with you, month after month, year after year. Feel the silence, the presence, the warmth underneath the words, in-between the words, surrounding the words, holding the words.

Let go of the destination. Savour the ever-changing seasons of your journey. Be present to each step. Remember to breathe.

Know that you do not walk alone.

With love,

Jeff Foster

Brighton, England
September 2013

… it is so precious, just to be able to sit in this open space together, where nothing needs to be resolved or solved; where we don't need to fix ourselves or be fixed; where our burning questions don't need to be answered; where, finally, our questions are allowed to just be questions; where our uncertainty doesn't need to be transformed into certainty; where our doubts are finally given permission to just be doubts. Here, in this warm embrace that we are, in this place of true meditation without a meditator, without a destination, without a controller, we don't need to find the answers, we don't need to come to any mental conclusions about life, we don't need to work everything out, we don't need to 'know', because finally, all our wondering and our wandering, our *trying-to work-it-all-out* and our *trying-to-make-it-all-work*, our exhausting seeking and searching and our desperation to find answers, is all just allowed to be here, exactly as it is…

– Jeff Foster, from a retreat in Glastonbury, England, 2012

JANUARY

Ever since happiness heard your name,

it has been running through the streets

trying to find you...

– Hafiz

THERE IS NOTHING WRONG WITH YOU

Friend, from the very beginning, you were not broken. You were not born into sin. You were not destined for the garbage heap. There was never anything fundamentally missing from your life. You just *thought* that there was. Others tried to convince you that you were not good enough, because they too felt not good enough. In your innocence, and with no evidence to the contrary, you believed them. So you spent all those years trying to fix, purify and perfect yourself. You sought power, wealth, fame and even spiritual enlightenment to prove your worth as a 'me'. You played the Build-A-Better-Me game, comparing yourself to other versions of 'me', and always feeling inferior or superior, and it all became so exhausting, trying to reach those unreachable goals, trying to live up to some image that you didn't even fully believe in anyway, and you longed for the deep rest of yourself...

But you were always perfect, you see, from the very beginning. Perfect in your absolute imperfection.

Your imperfections, your quirks, your seeming flaws, your weirdnesses, your unique and irreplaceable flavours, were what made you so loveable, so human, so real, so relatable. Even in your glorious imperfection, you were always a perfect expression of life, a beloved child of the universe, a complete work of art, unique in all the world and deserving of all the riches of life.

It was never about being a perfect 'me'. It was always about being perfectly Here, perfectly yourself, in all your divine strangeness.

"Forget your perfect offering," sings Leonard Cohen. "There is a crack in everything. That's how the light gets in."

A LOVING PROMISE

"I will always listen deeply to you, but I will never try to fix you, mend you, stop you feeling what you are feeling or give you second-hand, memorised answers. I will never pretend to be 'the one who knows', 'the enlightened one' or some missionary for a conceptual truth so far removed from real-time, immediate, first-hand present experience. I will not get into drama with you, I will not indulge and feed your stories and mental conclusions and fears, I will not mistake who you are for my story about you, my dream of who you are.

But friend, I will meet you in the fires of hell, I will hold your hand there, I will walk with you as far as you need to walk, and not turn away, for you are myself, and in the deepest recesses of our experience we are intimately each other, and we cannot pretend otherwise.

And so, if you feel confused, feel confused now. If you feel frightened, feel frightened now. If you are bored, let's get profoundly bored together. If you are burning with rage, let's burn together awhile and see what happens."

When we break the mould, interrupt the outdated pattern, and make the unexpected commitment to dignify our present experience by radically connecting with what's really here, without judging it or pushing it away, perhaps great healing is possible.

On every page of a book, behind the words – no matter what the words are describing, no matter what is going on in the story – there is the whiteness of the paper. Rarely noticed, even more rarely appreciated, but absolutely essential, so that the words can be seen.

The paper itself is not affected by the story that is being told – it is only there to hold the words, without condition. A love story, a war epic, a gentle comedy – the paper itself doesn't mind.

The paper does not fear the ending of the story, nor does it long for an earlier time in the story. The middle pages do not need to know how the story ends, and the final page does not mourn when the main character dies. The paper doesn't even know that the story is 'over'. The paper holds time but is not bound by time.

You don't know how many pages are left in the book of your life. You don't know how this autobiography will end. From the perspective of the mind, 'your life' is not yet complete, and thought is constantly trying to work out how to end your story in the best way. How to solve things, neatly? How to resolve the unresolved problems? How to tie up all the loose ends? How to fix everything?

But from the perspective of the paper – that is, from the perspective of your true identity as consciousness itself – life is forever complete as it is, and there is nothing to resolve, and the unknowability of things is their resolution. The story does not need to be 'completed' in the future for consciousness to be fully present now.

The paper simply meets the words exactly as they are.

From the perspective of the paper, even if the story is an epic one, from the first page to the last page, nothing has actually happened at all. The entire story has unfolded in perfect, unchanging stillness. The most incredible story never told.

Okay. So you feel peaceful, blissed out, in the flow. You're manifesting perfectly and life is going to plan. You're okay with everything that happens. You can't imagine ever suffering again.

Cut to the next scene in the movie of your life. There's been some kind of loss, shock, bolt of lightning from the blue. You're lying in bed, sick with pain, or grief, or despair. This was unexpected, unplanned. You've tried everything. Nothing's working.

Where did your awakening go? Weren't you supposed to be the one who was okay with everything, who met every experience with equanimity and an "effortless yes"? Where did all your spiritual progress go?

The spiritual 'me' feels humiliated and beaten up. Were you a fake, a fraud, a liar? Were you always kidding yourself? How do you get back to where you were?

Don't go back. Stay with it. You're awakening from another dream. The dream that present experience could or should conform to *any* image or expectation. You're discovering your own inner authority.

This scene is not a mistake. The movie of your life is not broken. You're rediscovering how vast you are, how much you can hold.

You don't have to feel 'okay' all the time. You don't have to be free from all resistance all the time. You are bigger than that, unlimited in fact. There is no 'all the time' for you. You are the space for the okay and the not-okay, the acceptance and the resistance. You don't need any fixed and unchangeable image of yourself. You don't need to be the *enlightened guru* or the *spiritual warrior*. You don't need to be *the peaceful one, the awakened one, the strong one, the highly evolved one, the one immune to suffering.* All are false limitations on your limitless nature. Simply be what you are, not 'this' one nor 'that' one, but The One, the space for all of it.

Let life kick you off your pedestal time and time again, until you lose all interest in being on pedestals.

BE GLORIOUSLY UNRESOLVED

You'll never reach a point in your life where everything is solved, all neatly tied up in a bow. That's the point. There's no 'final scene', only the on-going adventure movie, forever unresolved. You learn to love the mess of your life, its constantly changing nature, its unpredictability. And you stand as the immutable silence in the midst of the storm, the wide open space in which joy and pain, ecstasy and agony, boredom and bliss, can arise and subside like waves in the ocean. There are no problems when you know yourself as the space for it all.

TRUE ACCEPTANCE

Saying *yes* to this moment, exactly as it is, saying *yes* to yourself, exactly as you are, doesn't mean giving up on the possibility of change. It doesn't mean that answers won't arrive, that sadness won't disappear, that pain won't ease, that intelligent action won't happen in the next scene. It means a total alignment with the present scene, which contains the intelligence of an entire universe. It means deep trust in this instant of life – the only instant there is – and letting go of promises, and ideas of how life 'should' be.

Instead of trying to skip to tomorrow's certainty, trust the uncertainty of today. Instead of rushing towards an answer in the next scene, trust this creative scene of 'no answers yet'. Instead of trying to run towards joy or bliss in the future, trust this present moment of sorrow or doubt, or whatever shape the cosmic intelligence is taking. Certainty may or may not come in time, answers may arrive, joy may burst forth or not, thrilling moments may present themselves sooner or later, but don't skip over the treasures of this moment.

If answers come, they will emerge from the fertiliser of not knowing, the rich soil of doubt. If joy shows her face, she will emerge from pain that has been touched deeply. If a new life grows, it will grow in the only birthplace there is: *Now*.

This moment is the access point, the portal, the gateway of grace to all that you have ever longed for. Don't skip over it in pursuit of tomorrow's imagined glories.

I AM...

Be mindful about what you say after you say "**I Am...**" Those two tiny words contain powerful magic.

Language tries to fix you in time and space. It is an attempt to press *pause* on the ever-changing dance that you naturally are. In reality, what you truly are can't be fixed or captured or even put into words, for you are alive and dynamic and naturally immune to all fixed definitions.

For example: "I am sorrow"? "I am a sorrowful person"? "Sorrow defines me" "I am a victim of sorrow"? No. A wave of sorrow is arising in the vast ocean that you are, an ocean that cannot be defined by either 'happy' or 'sad' or anything in-between, but allows all those feelings to come and go.

You are not sorrow – sorrow comes and goes in you. You'll find no sorrowful person, no sorrowful entity, no sorrowful 'thing', no sorrowful 'me' here, only the energy of sorrow arising presently, energy that will dissipate as it is allowed to move. You are not sorrowful – you are the home for sorrow in this moment. You are not angry – you are the capacity for anger right now. You are not enlightened, ignorant, successful, a failure or a waste of space – you are all of this, and none of it. You are infinite potential, a sentence that never needs to be completed.

Use your magic wisely. Fall in love with being an ever-deepening mystery to yourself. Don't attempt to turn yourself into stone.

NOTHING IS WAITING

Today is not some insignificant stepping stone towards a glorious future performance on the stage. This moment is not life waiting to happen, goals waiting to be achieved, words waiting to be spoken, connections waiting to be made, regrets waiting to evaporate, aliveness waiting to be felt, enlightenment waiting to be gained.

No. Nothing is waiting. This is it. This moment is life. Not nearly life, not almost life, not conceptual life learned through repetition, but raw life living itself, exploding in fullness, radically present, dripping from every nook and cranny, bursting forth in motion and in rest – *life, life, life!* And it is yours to be tasted *now, now, now!*

Life is no trailer, no preview, no coming attraction. What you long for has already arrived, and it announces itself in and as every sensation, every thought, every image, every moment of pain, boredom or bliss. It's there even in the longing for it – that's how intimate it is.

You stand on holy ground now, your birthplace, your resting place, your womb, your tomb. The show has already begun, and the spotlight is illuminating all.

There is no time for 'one day' when you are truly alive, and today is the only day you'll ever truly live, if you are to live another day.

AN INVITATION

I don't want to hear what you believe
I'm not at all interested in your certainty
I couldn't care less about your unexcelled perfection

Share with me your doubts
Open up your tender heart
Let me in to your struggles

I'll meet you in that place
Where your spiritual conclusions
Are starting to crack open

That's where the creativity lies
That's where the newness shines
That's where we can truly meet:
Beyond the image

Your imperfections
Are so perfect
In this light

I don't want you to be perfect
I want you to be real

THE PATH

There is no fixed path to enlightenment. Enlightenment is not a destination, a goal, the final resting place at the end of a long journey – that's the mind's version of enlightenment. Enlightenment is infinitely closer than anything you could imagine.

This is very good news. It means that nobody is the authority on your path – no teacher, no guru, no religious leader. It means that nobody can tell you the right 'way' for you. It means that you cannot go wrong, even if you think you've gone wrong. It means that nothing that happens can ever lead you off the path, for the path *is* whatever happens.

Nothing can take you away from the miracle of life, or bring you closer to it for that matter, since the miracle is all around, already shining brightly, as every thought, sensation, image, feeling, smell, sound, and as the deeper miracle of the one who is aware of all this, intimate with all this, present to all this.

Be the light of awareness that you naturally are, enlightening the moment, whatever its contents. Doubt, fear, sadness, anger, intense confusion – maybe, just maybe, these are neither enemies nor blocks to enlightenment, but expressions of a deeper intelligence, the same incomprehensibly vast and awake intelligence that gives birth to stars and moves the ocean tides and sends each and every living thing off on its paradoxical journey towards its own being.

Shine your light on all that arises. Come out of the story of time and space and progression towards a future goal, and trust a sacred moment. Take any moment. Any moment at all, for any moment is the access point. There are never any blocks – only portals.

You are not some separate entity on a long journey towards a future completion.

You are pure poetry.

IN SAFE HANDS

You get tired of half-truths, don't you?
You get tired of pretending
You get tired of the world's promises
You get tired of... waiting.
You even get tired of getting tired.
You get tired of 'you' –
The one who 'gets tired of'.

A divine disillusionment
And a great paradox –
For who gets tired of whom?

And in the midst of despair
You find yourself staring life in the face
Naked and unprotected in front of its sacredness.

And for the first time
(For whatever reason)
You do not turn away.

It breaks you open
It shatters your dreams
It burns up your certainty.
Even your dreams of enlightenment
do not stand a chance.

You tremble with fear
You cry out for help
(Why has it forsaken you?)

And then
For the first time
You feel deeply alive
Undivided from the sacredness
Resting in the arms of the One you always sought
Unprotected yet utterly safe
Free at last
Free at last.

It destroys the one you thought you were
But it never touches the One you are.

This is the road less travelled.
A road leading not to the future
Not to the Promised Land
But to the one reading these words now

To the one who knew all along
That all along this road's ancient edges
Lie the shed skins of lost identities and unkept promises.

Clean yourself up, my friend
You were always in safe hands.

THE PRESENT MOMENT

I love being in the present moment. It is my true Home.

Now is the only place where I ever am. I always find myself Here, never coming, never going.

Yes, I have known the passing of thought and emotion, the arising and dissolving of states and experiences both ecstatic and mundane, but I have never known the passing of myself, That which never passes as everything passes. And so anywhere other than Now feels like homesickness and disconnection, death and decay. "Anywhere else" is a fantasy, anyway, for I cannot split myself from myself, look at myself from a distance and say "there I am!".

Any thought, sensation, feeling, image, memory, dream, vision, has always appeared right here, where I am, where you are, the only place we truly 'meet'. But we are not two, and so we cannot 'meet' – we can only recognise our original intimacy prior to time and all ideas of 'meeting'.

Beyond our stories, beyond our histories and future plans, this is the One place where we can never be apart. Here and Now.

SACRED DIS-ILLUSIONMENT

There are two core fears: losing what you have, and not getting what you want.

There is one solution: *Falling in love with where you are.*

We eventually realise that our partners, jobs, religions, possessions, trophies, bank balances, the fancy certificates on our walls, even our perfect bodies, won't make us happy. Not permanently or completely happy anyway, not the kind of ever-present happiness we truly seek and know is possible.

This realisation is dis-*illusion*-ment, the breaking-up of illusions, the falling away of childhood dreams, and it often manifests as depression, anxiety, existential nausea, despair, mid-life crises and addictions.

But disillusionment can be a wonderful thing. For contained within its sacred core is an invitation to go beyond all those worldly comforts and pleasures that never really delivered what they promised, and rediscover That which never changes – our true nature, our true *content*-ment prior to the ever-changing external *content* of our lives, prior to the bodymind.

When you realise that nothing, no external "thing" – no person, no object, no substance, no circumstance, no revelation, no single experience – ever has the power to make you permanently happy, you discover a deeper invitation: to realise that nothing, the no-thing that you are, *is* the source of true happiness, and that *every* experience holds the key.

Nothing can make you happy, therefore happiness lies within, and that is a reason for great joy.

LIFE IS AN ALTAR

You will lose everything. Your money, your power, your fame, your success, perhaps even your memories. Your looks will diminish. Loved ones will die. Your body will fall apart. Everything that seems permanent is in truth impermanent and will be smashed. Experience will gradually, or not so gradually, strip away everything that it can strip away. Waking up means facing this reality with open eyes.

But right now, in this very moment, you stand on sacred and holy ground, for that which will be lost has not yet been lost, and realising this simple thing is the key to unspeakable joy. Whoever or whatever is in your life right now has not yet been taken away from you. Everything is present.

The universal law of impermanence has already rendered everything and everyone around you so deeply holy and significant and worthy of your heart-breaking gratitude.

Loss has already transfigured your life into an altar.

THE DANCE

We never rehearsed this
We are a mess

We tremble and perspire
We step on each other's toes

Sometimes we go out of tune
And forget our lines

But at least this is real
At least we are not half-alive

Buried under the weight of some image
We never believed in anyway

I will always take this imperfect dance
Over no dance at all

FEBRUARY

The miracle is not to walk on water.

The miracle is to walk on this earth.

– Thich Nhat Hanh

THE GOOD NEWS

Right here, right now, in this moment, you don't have to 'figure out' the rest of your life, no matter what anyone says.

In this moment, you don't need all the answers. They will come, in time, or not, or perhaps the unnecessary questions will fall away.

There is no rush. Life is not in a hurry.

Be like the seasons. Winter is not trying to become summer. Spring does not rush towards autumn. The grass grows at its own pace. Even the rain is not rushing towards the ground.

The choices that will be made will be made, and you've no choice about that right now. The decisions that will happen will happen, events will unfold in time, but right now perhaps you don't need to know the solutions or the outcomes or how best to proceed. Perhaps *not knowing* is a welcome guest at life's banquet. Perhaps openness to possibility is a beloved friend. Perhaps even confusion can come to rest here, where you are.

And so, instead of trying to 'fix' our lives, instead of trying to neatly resolve the unresolvable and quickly complete the epic story of a fictitious 'me', we simply relax into utter not knowing, allowing everything to be 'out of control', trusting the order within the wild chaos, unravelling in the warm embrace of mystery, sinking deeply into the moment, savouring it fully, in all its uniqueness and wonder.

And then, perhaps without any effort, without any struggle or stress, without 'you' being involved at all, the true answers will emerge in their own sweet time.

Why run towards answers, when the questions themselves are such miracles?

One thing we all eventually learn, the hard way:

Never try to help someone unless they are ready to be helped.

Until help is asked for, until there is that readiness to listen and let go of old patterns, your attempt to help will be felt as manipulation and control – your issue, your need, not theirs. Defences will go up, positions will become hardened, you will end up feeling frustrated or superior or powerless, and the mirrored roles of 'victim' and 'saviour' will make you feel more disconnected from each other than ever.

How to truly help? Meet them where they are right now. Let go of your dream of their immediate healing. Slow down. Validate their present experience. Don't try to impose your own agenda or assume what is 'best' for them. Perhaps you don't know what is 'best'. Perhaps they are more hardy, intelligent, resourceful, and full of potential, than you ever thought possible.

Perhaps what is 'best' for them right now is not to want – or need – your help! Perhaps they actually need to suffer or struggle more. Perhaps they are aligning and healing in their own unique way. Perhaps what this moment requires is trust, and deep listening, and profound respect for where they are in their journey. Perhaps you are only trying to help yourself.

Perhaps real change comes not from trying to impose change on others, but from aligning with where they are right now, unlocking all the creative intelligence of the moment, honouring their unique path and their mysterious process of healing.

When you try to change someone, you are communicating to them that they are not okay as they are, that you reject and resist and dislike their present experience and want it to be different. You may even be communicating to them that you don't love them. When you stop trying to change them, and meet them as they are, and align with life as it presents itself, great and unexpected change is then possible, for now you are a true friend and ally of the universe.

Stop trying to change others, and they change, or not, in their own way, in their own sweet time.

Perhaps you help the most when you get out of help's way.

WHEN THE GROUND FALLS

What happens when the ground beneath your feet gives way?

A relationship ends unexpectedly, success turns to failure overnight, a loved one dies, you receive a diagnosis out of the blue, and you suddenly feel a profound groundlessness, a deep uncertainty, the sense that your world is spinning out of control. Nothing feels real anymore. It feels like your life is no longer 'your' life, like you're in some strange kind of impersonal movie, like you don't know where to turn, or even stand. The future, which once seemed so solid and 'real', is now exposed for the lie and the fairy story that it was, and your dreams of 'tomorrow' crumble to dust. 'Tomorrow' was never going to happen, not in the way you had unconsciously planned, anyway. There are no answers that will satisfy now, no authorities to guide you, since nobody can experience your experience for you, and nobody has the answers you need, and you feel profoundly alone on a tiny planet spinning in vast and unfathomable space. You feel like crawling back into the womb, but the womb has disappeared.

Wonderful! Oh, wonderful! What an invitation this is! Life has not gone wrong, for life cannot go wrong, for all is life, and life is all. Only our dreams and plans 'about' life can crumble, but life itself cannot. This present experience, this confusion and cosmic doubt, this heartbreak, is not against life, this *is* life, raging life, vibrant life, the sacred life of the moment. This is not the 'wrong' scene in the movie, this *is* the movie, however hard that is to see right now.

There is a vast intelligence at work here, an intelligence that breathes us at night, and beats our heart, pumps blood around the body, and heals our wounds when 'we' are not even around to notice or care.

What happens, when, just for a moment, we stop trying to

figure it all out, we stop clinging to the old dreams and stop mourning their loss, and we face the raw, broken-open reality of things as they are? What happens when, just for a moment, we actually take the radical and unexpected step of saying *yes* to the uncertainty, the doubt, the confusion, the pain, the heartbreak? What happens when we affirm the unsolved mystery instead of trying to escape it? What happens when we turn towards the devastation rather than away from it? What happens when we actually trust the broken-openness of things, and allow the deep intelligence of life to work its magic through the guise of devastation?

Can it be okay, just for a moment, to not have the answers, to not have the reference points, to not know anything anymore? Can it be okay, just for a moment, to feel *this*, whatever shape *this* is taking now? And in the midst of the rubble, can we once again breathe, and contact that place within ourselves, that most intimate and familiar place of silence and deep presence? The place that doesn't need to know and doesn't care about the outcome of dreams and doesn't want any answers? Can we remember that stillness that has secretly always been our best friend? Can we relax into that clarity which has never left? Can we take our stand as that awareness that cannot be destroyed?

Perhaps the cosmic intelligence that we are has not actually abandoned us, and right at the heart of the seeming mess of this moment, there is something that is not involved in the mess at all. We can call it love, or God, or consciousness, or simply Who We Really Are, prior to our dreams of how life should be, of how this moment should look and feel and taste and sound and smell. Perhaps our dreams are there to be broken, and our plans are there to crumble, and our tomorrows are there to dissolve into todays, and perhaps all of this is one giant invitation to wake up from the illusion of control and embrace whole-heartedly what is present.

Perhaps it is all a call to compassion, to a deep embrace of this universe in all its bliss and pain and bitter-sweet glory. Perhaps we were never really in control of our lives, and perhaps we are constantly invited to remember this, since we constantly forget it. Perhaps suffering is not the enemy at all, and at its core, there is a first-hand, real-time lesson we must all learn, if we are to be truly human, and truly divine. Perhaps *breakdown* always contains the seeds of *breakthrough*.

Perhaps suffering is simply a rite of passage, not a test or a punishment, nor a signpost to something in the future or past, but a direct pointer to the mystery of existence itself, here and now.

Perhaps our lives cannot go 'wrong' at all.

REWIND, PLAY, FAST-FORWARD

Regret is thought's futile attempt to alter the past. But trying to manipulate the past is like trying to rewind to, and alter, a previous scene in a movie you've already been watching for a while. Thought says "that scene should have been different!" or even "that scene shouldn't have happened at all!" But of course, the movie was perfect as it was – a perfection which actually included any seemingly 'imperfect' scenes. The appearance of past imperfection is part of the cosmic perfection of this moment.

The recognition that things are exactly as they are right now is not a call to detachment and life-denial, an excuse to dismiss the appearance of the world as 'illusory' with an uncaring attitude. Quite the opposite. We don't just sit back from life and say "everything is perfect so I'll do nothing to help or change things anymore." That is another blockage, another conceptual position, another escape from reality. This perfection is radically open to the world, open to the rest of the movie, open to what happens. We can still learn the lessons from the past, and take them into the future. But our sense of regret is gone. We no longer rewind. We could call this "trust", but there's no need to name it at all.

We cannot change the past (*Rewind*), we cannot know the future (*Fast-forward*), but we can meet life exactly as it is (*Play*), and play, and play...

ARE THERE TWO OF YOU?

You are a King, a Queen, watching over your magnificent ever-changing kingdom. Thoughts, sensations and feelings are constantly parading for you in the present moment. Without your constant Presence, there is no parade. Without You, there is nothing.

The one thing that you long for, the one thing you have always been seeking – YOU – is the one thing that will never appear in the parade of thought and emotion, for it cannot be a 'thing' to you. Thoughts will dance, sensations will tingle, feelings will burn, but You will never appear in your own presence – FOR THERE CANNOT BE TWO OF YOU. You could wait forever for You to appear. But who would be waiting?

From one perspective, this is a tragedy! You will never find what you seek through seeking it. The spiritual search therefore can end in exhaustion and disillusionment, frustration and even despair.

From another perspective the realisation that YOU CAN NEVER APPEAR TO YOU is a massive invitation to remember who you truly are prior to the parade: That which never appears or disappears, That without which no parade is possible, That which is beyond the endless cycle of birth, death and rebirth.

You are a King, a Queen, and there is no lineage, no line of succession – only You. This isn't narcissism or solipsism – this is deep peace, and heart-busted-open-compassion for all who do not yet understand their true worth.

THE PROMISE

In this presence beyond presence,
In this place that is no place at all,
In this warm embrace I call myself,
Even a 'no' is a secret yes,
Even resistance is deeply allowed,
Even doubt is a celebration of life.

Come, all you unloved creatures,
All you homeless waves in life's vast ocean,
Pain, doubt, shame, guilt,
All you frightened orphans of light,
Crawl out of your hiding places,
Shuffle out of the darkness,
You are invited to a great feast.

Come, uncertainty, sit by my side,
Come, despair, drink from my cup,
Come, fear, do not be afraid of me,
I will not turn away from you,
I will not deny you a place at this table,
Now that I know the truth of myself.

I invited you here, long ago.
I have an ancient promise to keep.

A CELEBRATION OF WEIRD

Don't become a spiritual zombie, devoid of passion and deep human feeling.

Let spirituality become a celebration of your uniqueness rather than a repression of it. Never lose your quirkiness, your strangeness, your weirdness – your unique and irreplaceable flavour. Don't try or pretend to be 'no-one' or 'nothing' or some transcendent and impersonal non-entity with 'no self' or 'no ego', 'beyond the human' – that's just another conceptual fixation and nobody's buying it any more.

Be a celebration of what your unique expression is and stop apologising. Fall in love with this perfectly divine, very human mess that you are.

There is no authority here, and no way to get life wrong. So get it all wrong.

Fail, gloriously.

THE MEDICINE OF DESPAIR

I often get excited when someone reports uncaused and seemingly inexplicable sadness. I see sadness, like all the other waves in the ocean of life, as an invitation, an invocation, a calling to open up to deeper truths about existence, to recognise our inherent vastness.

Life is bitter-sweet. However beautiful things are right now, they will pass. Everything is impermanent and groundless. You will die, at least in this incarnation. Everyone you love will pass on. Your success may turn to failure. What you have, you may lose. Your body will cease to function in the way it does now. Nothing is certain, everything is cast into doubt. The water of relative existence slips through our fingers so easily. Our joy is tinged with sadness. Our bliss is pierced with nostalgia. The yin and the yang of things won't let you settle on an independent opposite. There is no home for the homeless here.

Contacting this deeper truth of existence, encountering the raw ground of being unprotected and unprepared may initially present as melancholy and even despair, but that existential disturbance may contain unlimited riches.

At the point of despair, when the ground falls away from under our feet and life spins out of control (were we ever 'in' control?), often we are medicated, or we self-medicate, with pills or sex or alcohol or even spiritual teachings. Science would like to reduce our existential predicament to the dysfunction of brain chemicals, easily remedied with a few innocent-looking pills prescribed by someone with a hard-won certificate. And perhaps those theories have some validity – through certain lenses. But there are so many other lenses. Infinite lenses. There are myriad sides to this diamond of human experience, and it would be a shame to reduce our glorious being to chemicals or neurons.

Perhaps our depression is not a sickness (though I will never argue with anyone who wants to defend that view) but a call to break out, to let go, to lose the old structures and stories, perspectives and opinions we have been holding about ourselves and the world and rest deeply in the truth of who we really are.

Conventional wisdom would have you turn away from melancholy rather than face it. Well-meaning friends and family and self-help gurus may want to fix you, to get you 'back to normal' (what the hell is normal, anyway?), to make you more 'positive', to cheer you up. What if 'normal' no longer fits? What if you need to shed your half-shed skin, not climb back into it? What if sadness, and pain, and fear, and all of the waves in life's ocean, just want to move in you, to finally express themselves creatively and not be pushed away? What if you are tired of being average?

What if you are not nearly as limited as you were led to believe? What if you are vast enough to hold and contain all of life's energies, the 'positive' and the 'negative'? What if you are beyond both, an ocean of consciousness, unified, boundless and free, in which even the deepest despair has a resting place?

What if your depression was simply your infinite intelligence calling you back Home, in the only way it knew how?

Your melancholy may contain natural medicine.

THE END OF SEPARATION

Nobody you have loved has ever left you. They only buried them-selves so deeply in your heart that it was hard to recognise them for a while.

When our imagined boundaries begin to melt, when the protective walls around our tender hearts soften, our loved ones breathe again, and come out of the darkness. When you have been touched by someone, felt the warmth of their presence, even if it was only for a moment and so long ago, you are forever changed, and cannot go back or forget, however strongly you build those defences. Once you know the presence of God you can never be the same.

In the Bible it is written: "The mountains will be overturned, the cliffs will fall, and every wall will crumble to the ground." In presence, in the fullness of Now, separation cannot stand. Love does not know time nor limitation. It is beyond death.

THE SMELL OF STRUGGLE

Here is an ancient invitation to love the struggle of life, the sorrow, the confusion, the uncertainty, even the despair of it. Love the impermanence of it all, love it all to death, its unpredictability, its uncontrollability, its unmanageable quality and mysterious nature.

Life was never supposed to be 100% smooth. What would be the fun in the ride? Love the bumps along the way. Love the total absence of any answers that satisfy. Love your own inability to love sometimes. There are never any mistakes here in this place we call reality, and nothing is thrown at you except rich and nutrient-dense fertiliser, which may smell bad at first, and you may be tempted to run away, but its smell contains a secret: it will lovingly help new things grow, if you give it a chance and stop assuming it is divided from the supreme intelligence of life itself, the One intelligence that births solar systems and tiny birds in springtime. The smell of your struggle is the smell of life, not death, and does not indicate your terrible failure, but your stunning aliveness. Yes, yes, you are alive, and sensitive, and you feel everything!

Waking up doesn't mean 'being okay' with everything all the time, or 'being fearless' all the time, or 'being relaxed' all the time, or being anything 'all the time' for that matter, for why would you place such heavy demands on present experience? Why would you put conditions on the unconditional, and whose conditions would they be anyway? Why would you want to live up to a second-hand, time-bound image?

Thankfully, what you are never has to live up to any image of how awakening 'should' look. The myriad, ever-moving waves in the ocean of you can't be anything 'all the time' since they are alive – they love to dance and play and arise and dissolve as spontaneously as they arose, leaving no trace – and this recognition is the beginning of such cosmic relief for the exhausted seeker of 'the next experience'.

Life never has to match up to your idea of 'life' and that's why life is so restful at its very core. There is simply no demand for present experience to be anything other than what it is. There is simply *this* – present, complete, empty and full.

But, intelligent and discerning reader, this inherent perfection does not equate to detachment and apathy. Quite the opposite! It's not 'just letting things be' or doing 'doing nothing' or preaching 'there is no me' to anyone who will listen. It's not a mental conclusion or second-hand belief, or a way to block out pain. It's more of a living attitude, a way of being, a seeing that, no matter what arises in present experience – a thought, a sensation, a feeling – no matter how intense or unexpected, these visitors have a home in you, they are welcome as beloved and inseparable waves of yourself. Love is no longer a fancy notion but a living, breathing, real-time reality. The poets and sages were right. The end of violence is here within you. And from this creative and compassionate place we become more engaged with life than ever, more alive than ever, even as all stories and dreams of 'my life' and 'how it should be' fall away.

This love, this deep and ever-present silence that you are, is so vast it swallows everything. It pays no heed to images of how it should be. It does not try to impress, it is not looking for rewards, acceptance or validation. It is not pretending to be transcendent, or fearless, or beyond pain, it has no use for the word 'spiritual' or 'enlightened', it does not act as if it's above everything. It knows no bypassing, no clever tricks, no ways to numb itself to itself. It gets its hands dirty.

Yes, this is a dirty love. The unloved and unwanted and unmet get stuck under its fingernails. It wants all of its children, not just the pretty ones. It is the mother, the father, the lover, the guru we have always longed for. It loves because that's all it knows. It would work its knuckles to the bone just to be here.

We pretend to be fearless and beyond human concerns only because we are afraid. We act at being peaceful and undisturbed only because there is a storm inside. We strain to show others how far beyond anger we have gone, only because anger still rages in us, longing to be met. We show off our perfect spiritual know-ledge in public to mask our perfect private doubt. It's a perfect balance.

Who will stop pretending? Who will meet the 'shadow', the misunderstood 'dark side' of life, those waves of ourselves that are not inherently negative or sinful or dark, just neglected and abandoned and longing for home? Who will meet life's orphaned children? Who will sacrifice the image for the delight of not knowing?

It is such a relief to no longer have to pretend to be any-thing – not 'the awakened one', nor 'the one who knows', nor 'the blissed-out experiencer', nor 'the spiritual expert' – and instead to know ourselves on a deeper level as the home for those homeless parts of experience that we always thought 'should' disappear.

Our unwanted children cannot disappear until they are truly free to appear in us. And when they are truly free, who would ever want them to disappear? When they are no longer unwanted, is there any problem? Even the unwanted are wanted here in the vastness that we are. There is plenty of space.

Beyond awakening, there is this grace, this inexplicable and heart-breaking timeless welcoming of everything as it arises. By dirtying itself until it cannot dirty itself any more, love purifies itself.

FORGET PERFECTION

Forget trying to get it "right" all of the time.

Here's to doing your best, falling flat on your face, getting up again, falling down again, screwing up totally, failing beyond belief, being laughed at, ridiculed, mocked, even crucified, and losing what you thought was yours.

And here's to embracing the mess of it all, dying to the dream and waking to the reality of it, loving the perfect imperfection of it, opening your heart wide to all of it, continuing to live your truth despite everything, fearlessly meeting each sacred moment with open eyes.

You cannot get it "right", and that's why you cannot get it "wrong", and out beyond both, there is a field...

IN MY FATHER'S FIELD

In my father's field I stood
I felt his longing
For something he could not name

In my mother's old room
By her empty bed
In the place she used to dream
I felt her fragile heart
And her courage to open it
Just enough

In my brother's house
By the peeling wallpaper
In the room that was never quite complete
I finally understood
Why he never understood
And I wept myself clean

Father, mother, brother
Were you not as I was?
Trying to close a broken circle?
Seeking resolution?

Now, at last, the circle is unbroken
Now, at last, we meet

We're not so different, you and I.

MARCH

Since everything is only an illusion,

perfect in being what it is,

having nothing to do with good or bad,

acceptance or rejection,

one might as well burst out laughing!

– Longchenpa

UNIVERSAL LOVE

Before I am born, before I am 5 years old, 49 years old, 84 years old, before I die

Before I am a student, before I am a teacher, before I am an artist, a shopkeeper, a doctor, a monk, a priest, a farmer, a scientist, a spiritual seeker

Before I am a Christian or a Buddhist

Before I am good or bad, right or wrong

Before I am a success or a failure

Before I am enlightened or unenlightened

Before I am a man or a woman

Before I am this body or that body

Before I am anybody

Before I am "the one who knows"

Before I am "the one who doesn't know"

Before I am this or that

Before I am something

Before I am anything

I am.

This no-thing that allows every-thing,

This wide open space,

Unlimited, incomprehensible,

In which every thought, sensation, feeling, arises and subsides,

Like waves in the ocean,

Ever-present,

Unchanging.

I Am.

Life itself.

This mystery.

Creation, destruction.

Like a cloudburst in the vastness...

I am born. Absolute is relative. Time. Space. Expansion. Contraction. I breathe in and out. I suckle my mother's breast. I am 5 years old, 49 years old, 84 years old. I grow and learn. I am a student, teacher, artist, dancer, shopkeeper, doctor, mystic, monk, priest, farmer, scientist, adventurer, murderer, thief. I am a man. I am a woman. I am gay, straight, black, white, rich and poor, loved and unloved.

I am every mother, every father, every son, every daughter. I am every slave in ancient Rome. I am every child on the streets of Calcutta. I am every dying sun. The birth of every star.

I cannot ever be something without being nothing at all.

I cannot be nothing without being all there is.

This is crucifixion and resurrection.

This is love beyond understanding.

This is the heartbeat of the cosmos.

I am That.

HOW TO MEET HEARTBREAK

I was speaking with a friend who had suddenly lost someone very close to him. His heart was broken wide open. He felt raw, exposed, unprotected, vulnerable, devoid of answers, unable to comprehend the mysteries of birth and death and sudden loss, unable to comfort himself with clichés. Why do loved ones disappear overnight? Why does such beauty seem to vanish so quickly? Why is there such pain, and why is there such grace?

In search of answers, he had gone round the circuit of contemporary spiritual teachers, each of whom gave him a lecture about reality and what does or doesn't lie 'beyond'. One lectured about reincarnation, another about the experienceless experience of deep dreamless sleep, another about the soul's journey after death, another about the pure perfection of pure uncontaminated awareness, and another simply laughed at his questions and made him feel like an unenlightened fool. None of the answers spoke to his broken heart.

Who would meet him in the midst of this raging fire? Who would validate his burning pain and the loss of his dreams? Who would, just for one moment, stop lecturing at him, stop telling him what they knew or believed to be true, and simply meet him as he was? Who would stop hiding behind their role as 'spiritual expert' or 'perfect teacher', and allow their heart to break with him, just for one moment? Who was willing to be that unprotected, that vulnerable, that open to life and the loss of the image?

Friends, are we ready to stop pretending that we have the answers? Are we ready to end our ceaseless regurgitation of spiritual clichés ("there is no self", "nobody dies", "everything is perfect", "there is only Oneness"). Isn't it time for us to wake up from this dream of nonduality, to let go of these final crutches of ours, these last barriers to the raw, fragile, precious truth of existence, and truly meet the one in front of us?

For it is our sons, our daughters, our mothers and fathers, husbands, wives and beloved friends who have just dropped dead. We are only ever meeting ourselves, and our hearts break together, as they must. **No movement towards answers is necessary.** No second-hand formulae about reincarnation, karma, soul journeys and the existence or non-existence of the afterlife will hold up here. No teachers, no students, no personal specialness at all, will ever survive this furnace of intimacy.

The broken heart requires no lectures. So let us meet, now.

THE RAIN

What's worse, the falling rain, or your resistance to getting wet?
The changing winds, or your battle against them?
The grass as it grows, or your demand for it to grow faster?
This moment, or your rejection of it?
Consider the possibility that Life is never 'against' you.
You are Life.

ONLY CONNECT

On your deathbed, will you still care about all the arguments you won, about all the times you proved to others how 'right' or how 'enlightened' you were, about all the knowledge you amassed on your journey to this moment? Will you still be thinking about how much money you made or didn't make, or how far you advanced up the material or spiritual or social ladder?

Or perhaps only this moment will matter, only the grace of each and every breath, only the precious fragility of life itself and the gratitude for it having been at all.

Like the dream of a childhood Christmas long ago, perhaps you will not remember the size or shape or the monetary value of the gifts that life offered, or what the gifts were wrapped in, or who got a bigger or better gift than you. Perhaps you will only remember the love and the longing and the hope with which the gifts were given, and received.

It was only ever about the connection.

THE SCREEN OF ACCEPTANCE

No matter what happens in a movie, the movie screen is not affected. As the main character ages, the screen doesn't age. As time passes *on* the screen, time never passes *for* the screen. When the main character dies, the screen remains alive, and is not diminished. Even when the movie ends, the screen itself does not end, it just remains open for the next movie – a comedy, a horror, a romance, a silent movie from 1912, a three-dimensional blockbuster from 2014 – whatever it will be. The screen accepts it all unconditionally – movie or no movie at all. The screen never fights the movie, nor does it cling to it; that's how it's made, that's its nature. It has no name, no age, no identity of its own, but allows those wonderful identities to parade themselves about, asking nothing in return. It is rarely appreciated, often ignored, but absolutely essential for the relative dance of life. The screen is pure love, pure acceptance with no opposite. It is what you are.

THE ULTIMATE SACRIFICE

Speak your deepest truth, even if it means losing everything – your pride, your status, your image, even your way of life.

A life of lies and half-truths, the burden of unspoken things, will eventually suffocate you and everyone around you.

Give up everything for a truthful existence. Know that you can only lose what's non-essential.

MY WAY

Life does not always go 'my way'.
But 'I' never get in the way
Of life not going 'my way'.
So life always goes my way.

I am the way of life.
Whichever way life goes, I go.
There is no way
That I can be separate from life's way.

Life *is* the way.
So there is no 'way'.

Life does not always go 'my way'.
But 'I' never get in the way.
So life always goes my way.
Even when it doesn't.

BEYOND THE IMAGE

I find truth in anything anyone ever says about me, so nobody can be my psychological enemy. Call me a fraud, I can find it. Call me a liar, I can find it. Call me a horrible failure, I can find it. Call me unreasonable, irresponsible, ignorant, deluded, full of ego, totally unenlightened, the worst being in the world, I can find all of it.

Like you, I am an unlimited ocean of consciousness, ever-present and forever free, and every thought, every sensation, every feeling, every image, every dream, every sound, every smell, every fragile, gossamer-like appearance, transitory and beautiful, comes and goes like a wave in my unending embrace. As consciousness, I have nothing to hide, nothing to lose, no image to protect, and nothing to defend since nothing can threaten what I am. Everything dances in my presence. Every possible facet of experience is available to me, seen and held in what I am, and so I am profoundly connected to all humanity, and beyond. This recognition is truly the end of war, the end of protecting a mirage called 'me', the end of the defence of the false.

Next time you get triggered by someone's opinion of you, ask yourself this: "What am I defending? An image of myself? If I can be aware of that image right now, can it really be who I am?" This inquiry is the key to unimaginable peace.

Be grateful to anyone who has ever given you any kind of honest feedback. They are your gurus, one and all.

ANOTHER DAY

Stop, just for a moment, and consider this: You've been given another day on this earth.

Let your heart break into a million pieces today, if it wants to. Allow yourself to cry today, if tears come. Feel vulnerable today, if vulnerability visits. Allow all of life to move through you, if it moves today.

A taste. A glance. A breath. The touch of a loved one's hand. The vibrantly alive and familiar upsurge of joy or pain. This is a day of gratitude for the smallest and most 'insignificant' of happenings, even for those which seem unworthy of your gratitude.

This is not 'just another day'. This is your first day, and your last day. Your birth day and your death day. Your only day. Your longed-for day of grace.

THE COMMITMENT

What happens when, even when we feel like leaving, abandoning the moment for the promise of a future salvation, we stay, sitting with the raw, unfiltered, boundlessly alive life-energy that is simply trying to express right now? What happens when, just for a moment, we stay with our pain, our fear, our doubt, our discomfort, our grief, our broken heart, even our numbness, without trying to change it, or fix it, or numb ourselves to it, or get rid of it in any way? What happens when, just for a moment, despite all urges to the contrary, we don't "do" anything about our discomfort or grief, we drop all tricks and tactics and clever manipulations and, instead, we begin to deeply acknowledge what is here, saying hello to it, honouring its existence, listening to its deeper call, sinking into the mystery of it? What happens when we make the radical commitment to never turn away from this moment, as it dances in emptiness?

In reality, we are only ever given a moment of pain, and never more, although thought tries to project the pain into time, creating the story of "my past and future pain", moving into the epic movie of "my lifelong struggle with pain". But life itself is only ever a moment, and we are always spared from time itself. Can we meet the raw life energy as it arises right now? That is the question.

And who meets life? Is there anyone here separate from life in the first place? Is there any choice in the matter? Is there not just intimacy with all experience? Is the ultimate meeting not already happening? Am I not, as the ocean of consciousness, already totally inseparable from the waves of myself, the thoughts, sensations and feelings? Am I not already fully committed to these children of myself, these beloved expressions of my own blood and guts? Is this not an ancient devotion?

And so, it's not so much that we need to make a commitment to fearlessly contact our embodied experience. It's more a case of remembering this ancient promise that we already are. In the depths of our being, we are already fully devoted to being here. It is when we forget this primal commitment that we are, that we suffer and seek and long to return home.

"Move towards me", our grief whispers. "Just for a moment. Do not be afraid. I am made of you."

"But I don't know how to move", we reply.

"Then I shall move towards you. Do not be afraid. Here I come."

TO YOUR KNEES

Life will eventually bring you to your knees.

Either you'll be on your knees cursing the universe and begging for a different life, or you'll be brought to your knees by gratitude and awe, deeply embracing the life that you have, too overwhelmed by the beauty of it all to stand or even speak.

Either way, they're the same knees.

ON HOLY GROUND

They say to look upon God's face
Would be unbearable
We would be blinded by light

Then I have died a thousand times over
I have burnt at the stake of existence
All images of myself have melted

And even that cannot be true

I say 'God' but I have to laugh –
The word has lost all meaning
God is only a metaphor

For this fragile gift of a life
For this precious moment, unrepeatable
For this consciousness, unspeakable

For a familiar look on a stranger's face
For those icy winter branches
For each footstep, falling

There is no unholy ground

IN LOVE WITH LEPERS

Awakening is not a goal, nor is it a well-trodden path towards a fixed destination. It is not a personal achievement, nor an exclusive club for comfortable and well-read philosophers.

It is danger. It is falling madly in love with lepers. It is diving into mysterious waters.

A SILENT INTENTION

Perhaps it's time to stop trying to 'fix' the one in front of you, to stop trying to give them answers or solve their problems. You're not very good at that, friend. Your nature is not manipulation, but presence; not division, but wholeness.

Perhaps it's time to stop pretending to be the all-knowing authority, the infallible teacher, the fully-healed expert. Even with the best of intentions, you may unknowingly be interfering with their natural healing processes. You may be keeping them dependent on you, distracting them from a deep trust in their own first-hand experience.

Remember, they may need to feel worse before they feel better. They may need to feel their pain more deeply before they open up to their true source of healing. They may need to die to who they thought they were, before they can truly live. True for them, true for you.

So relax. Breathe. Come out of the drama. Acknowledge your desire to change or fix or even pacify them.

Now, simply listen without judgement, and try to understand where they are now. Stand in their shoes. See clearly who and what is in front of you.

Perhaps the greatest help you can offer right now is your clarity and non-judgemental attention – your natural compassion. Bring that transmission; be that presence; offer that openness. Stay wide open to solutions that have not yet been born. Trust life's strange processes. Be the silent intention – and the right words, actions, interventions, decisions, will come without effort.

Sanctify their moment by not running away. Mirror their own capacity to be present. Trust the ancient mystery of healing.

Perhaps the true medicine can flourish when 'you' get out of the way. Yes, drugs and good advice may numb or even remove symptoms, but an invitation to a deeper spiritual healing may be lurking just under the surface of things.

APRIL

There is a voice that doesn't use words.

Listen.

– Rumi

ON RECEIVING UNEXPECTED NEWS

You receive some unexpected news. You notice a sinking feeling in your stomach. The mind projects all kinds of pictures about how life 'could' or 'should' have been. It feels like life has gone wrong, like a dream is dying, like something that was yours has been lost. It all seems so wrong, so unfair, so cruel.

You start focussing on what is missing, what isn't here, what went away, what will never return. You no longer feel at home in the moment. You feel disconnected, isolated, separate, like you need some external circumstance to change for you to be at peace again, to once again find a stable equilibrium.

But wait. Nothing has died except a dream of how it was 'supposed to be'. But it *wasn't* going to be that way. Not now. It is *this* way, now.

Perhaps nothing has gone wrong in the universe at all, and this moment is not a mistake, not an enemy to be feared or rejected, but a friend, here to be honoured and embraced.

When the focus is on what's missing, what's gone, what's lost, we feel lost, homesick, ungrounded, separated from source, divided against ourselves, and 'a house divided against itself cannot stand'. The never-ending story of lack begins with present-moment resistance.

When the focus is on what's still here, and what never left, and what's always here – when we remember who we really are, presence itself – we know that nothing fundamental has been lost. We feel aligned again, back home, even in the midst of devastating news. Perhaps the news was not a mistake at all. Perhaps it was yet another invitation to align, to turn towards the moment, to breathe deeply, and to remember who we are, which is never lost, never absent, never truly forgotten, and never far away. It is our peace, our joy and our unshakeable strength, our deeply rooted tree in a raging storm.

LIFE'S EMBRACE

Your life situation doesn't need to be perfect. You don't need to be blissed-out all of the time. You don't always need to be certain, or right. You don't need to be at peace all the time, or joyful all the time. You don't need to be anything, in fact – since you are everything, and there is room for everything, here in the vast and unchanging ocean of Being that you are, an ocean that is radically open to all of those waves of experience as they arise and dissolve.

You are the backdrop of stillness in an ever-changing gossamer world, where nothing remains fixed and where all edges and boundaries are subject to decay and dissolution and mystery. You are what remains when all is gone, even the idea "all is gone" and "I am what remains".

What holds all of it, allows all of it? What cannot be doubted, even when there is doubt? Who is reading these words right now? Who or what is trying to understand them? This is not the perfection of the mind, not "the perfect life" or "the perfect body" or "the perfect experience" or even "the perfect moment", but the perfection that is the absolute embrace of all of this, exactly as it is – the perfect embrace that you already are.

THE FIERCEST GRACE

I was talking to a dying friend. He was having trouble breathing and was in a lot of pain. He was telling me how, despite the pain, it was all perfect somehow, in a way he couldn't explain. That in the midst of the blood and the sleepless nights and the immobility, he had found a place of serenity. A place of freedom from his story of himself as 'the dying one'. A place of freedom from all dreams and hopes for the future, and a deep acceptance of things as they were.

Life had radically simplified itself – the moment was all that mattered now, and all that had ever mattered. He told me, "Despite all this, I wouldn't swap this life for any other."

This was the kind of love they don't teach in books. This wasn't the conceptual love of the mind, nor the fluffy happy love that comes and goes and depends on things going 'my way', but an unconditional love, a blood and sweat love, a fierce and unyielding grace without a name, indestructible, forever renewing itself in the furnace of presence, blowing anything unreal before it to smithereens. Pain was my friend's final guru, whose lessons were brutal and unexpected but ultimately pointed to nothing less than his total spiritual freedom, his infinite nature, deathless and eternal.

UNBREAKABLE

What's wrong with falling apart?

Why not fall apart so completely that there's nothing left? And then keep falling apart for the rest of your life, recognising yourself as the wide open space of awareness that cannot fall apart, but deeply allows all falling apart to happen?

And then can you really call it 'falling apart' at all?

Thoroughly fallen apart, thoroughly One.

WHAT YOU REALLY WANT

You don't really want what you think you want
You only want your wanting to end
To no longer want for anything
To be existentially full and complete

But isn't that just another want?
Perhaps the biggest want of all?

"Want" actually means "lack"
So now the question changes:
What do you really *lack*?
Do you really lack anything in this moment?

Thought says *yes*
Thought lists all the things that are missing
Thought advises that certain objects, people, experiences would complete this moment
Thought is always a seeker
It is always comparing
Thought says: "If you get what you want
The lack will disappear permanently
And life will be complete"

Get what you want! No more lack!

Do you see the trick here?

A mechanism perfectly designed to keep you away from what you really want

What is true abundance?
It's not about getting what you want
It's not about filling an absence
It's about realising that the present moment never lacks anything
It's already full to the brim with sights and sounds and smells
With thoughts and feelings
With colours and shapes beyond imagination

A thought or feeling of lack
A sense of 'something missing'
Is actually part of this moment's completeness
Not a threat to it
Part of the richness of Now
Not an enemy
A welcome visitor in the vast open space that you are
An old friend, come for tea

Space lacks nothing
For it is full with everything
Pregnant with possibility
Rich with potential

The mind confuses peace with 'absence'

Space with 'emptiness'
And unlimited capacity with 'lack'
And the game is on
The search for opposites
The longing for goals

You don't really want what you think you want
And that's why getting what you want
Doesn't satisfy 'you' for long

Who you really are does not 'want' anything
It has never heard of 'lack'
It is already satisfied with this moment
For it is this moment
Exactly as it is

This is true abundance:
Remembering who you really are
Prior to time and change

These are the unparalleled riches of the universe:
A breath
The simple feeling of being alive

Getting what you thought you wanted
Acquiring all the material and spiritual riches of the universe
Doesn't even come close

When nothing belongs to you
Everything is yours

This moment is a strange and unexpected jackpot

A CONSTANT APOCALYPSE

For you, every day is the end of the world. Every hour, every minute, every moment, the old world is falling away, the known is burning itself up, and the new, the never-before-seen-world, is revealing itself, in all its freshness. Truly, every moment is the end of a dream, and the birth of newness.

Seen in the light of truth, life is a constant apocalypse, a constant awakening to what is, yet the separate self, with its fear of the loss of the status quo and its clinging to form and ideology, pushes 'apocalypse' into time, and even fixes it to a specific date. And when that date passes, the mechanism creates a new date. It has to. This has always been the case. It is the seeker in action. To the illusory self, the end of the world will always be 'nigh'. It's how it keeps its own illusion going. It loves the drama of it.

And all the while, this timeless, ever-present apocalypse has always been with us, sweetly singing its song of emergence and unshakeable truth.

STOP

Whatever is happening in the circumstances of your life, stop.

Gently begin to acknowledge what is here, in this moment.

Come out of your conclusions about life, your ideas about the past and future, and begin to notice the sensations, feelings, thoughts that are present, right here and right now. Notice what is alive and immediate here. Let your present experience – sights and sounds and smells – become totally fascinating, the most curious dance in all the universe. You are seeing, tasting, touching, hearing the world as if for the first time. This is your Garden of Eden, and you are awake to it at last.

Notice how thought is always giving names and labels to things. A car, a tree, a foot. It even labels what you are feeling – "sadness", "anger", "fear", "disappointment", "expectation" and so on. And then judges it as good or bad, right or wrong. Is the feeling the word? Is the judgement the feeling? Is the thought the reality?

Try the following as an experiment: Instead of calling it 'sadness', drop that label for a moment, and sink deeply into the raw sensation in the body. Feel deeply the sensation in the stomach, the chest, the heart, the throat, the back of the head. Assume that you don't even know that it's sadness yet. Allow that unnamed life energy to dance and move freely in the sacred space that you are.

Instead of calling it 'anger', drop that heavy and loaded word, and directly contact the intense raw sensation in the belly, chest, throat. Feel directly the intensity of it. Feel the sheer aliveness of it. You are alive! You are alive! Allow life to move without blockage. Notice that these waves of energy are already allowed, without you having to allow them. They are allowed because they are life.

Instead of calling it 'fear' – or 'boredom' or 'frustration' or 'powerlessness' – drop that second-hand conclusion, and directly contact the raw, first-hand sensation in the body. Is this energy really against you? Allow it to burn, fizzle, prickle, dance, move, as if for the first time. You have never met this energy before. It is fresh in this moment. Is it really a threat to life? Is it really blocking anything, except an *idea* of how this moment should be?

What is sadness, when it is not named? What is anger, when we no longer call it 'anger'? What is fear, prior to the word 'fear'? What happens when we profoundly contact these life energies without history?

A POEM FOR NO-ONE

Who has been wearing these shoes?
Who has been walking in these footsteps?
Who eats this breakfast?
Speaks these words? Breathes? Moves as I do?

Who has known both the mountains of bliss and the valleys of total disillusionment?

Who has journeyed into the abyss and come out unbroken on the other side?

Who has suffered both the joys of pain and the pains of ecstasy?

Who has never abandoned me, throughout nirvana, samsara and those unspeakable realms of light?

Who has taken the hand of the child, the unloved one, the frightened one, the dying one?

Who is both the lover and the beloved and the imaginary gulf between them?

Who has cradled the entire universe in its arms?

Who is closer than the most intimate sensation?

Who asks these questions that cannot ever be answered, and delights in asking them anyway?

Whose music is it that I hear from dawn until dusk?

Is it You who wears these shoes?

Is it You who breathes these dying breaths?

Is it You I return to?
Is it You I never left?

Once, in pursuit of You, I ran from You.
I ran from these shoes and from the surfaces of things.
I ran from all that I judged as mere 'appearance'.

I ran from the simple wonder of waking up in the morning to a fresh new day, not knowing what was to come.

But now, I run no more.
I can no longer seek, or escape, what I already am.
I have been gutted, turned inside out, replaced by gratitude,
and left not knowing why
I ever doubted this miracle
in the first place.

TIME TRAVEL

There is no such thing as a thought from the past. Who we really are does not 'travel' into the past in thought. A thought about the past, a memory, an image, arises in the present. A thought about the future, a dream of what may or may not happen, the imagination of a plan, does not happen in the future, it happens here, now. Past and future do not happen in the past or future – they arise here, where you are – just as a movie set in the past does not cause the movie screen to travel into the past.

This moment is not really a 'moment' separate from any other moment at all. It is not a sliver of time between a separate past and future moment. This moment is the vast field where stories of past and future arise and fall, where dreams are born and die, where thoughts, sensations, sounds, smells, feelings, all arise and dissolve, leaving no trace. This moment is vast and timeless and holds everything.

Since the words 'moment' and 'movement' come from the same root (Latin, *movere*) it may be better to call this the *present movement* of life. The movement of thoughts, sensations, feelings. The movement of past and future. And what is aware of all this movement? That which never moves. That which you truly are.

In the midst of all the movement of life, the total stillness of You.

PERFECTLY UNFINISHED

Perhaps your imperfections
Are not really 'imperfections'
And not 'yours' at all

Perhaps they are the last remnants
Of a greater perfection
Misunderstood by mind and forgotten long ago

Come out of the story of the 'poor me'
And discover the riches in the smallest of things
A single breath, a glance from a friend, an autumnal breeze

Celebrate the unwanted, the unloved stranger, the perfect
mistake

Collapse into wonderful unknowing

Be perfectly unfinished,

At last.

FALLING IN LOVE WITH WHERE YOU ARE

Dying to all
you think you know

Letting go of the image
of how life 'should' be

Sinking into the vast mystery
of the present moment

Embracing change and loss
as misunderstood friends

Falling in love
with where you are

This is the path
for those who know
there is no path

Only endless destinations
and never-ending beginnings

MAY

Once you realise that the road is the goal,

and that you are always on the road,

not to reach a goal, but to enjoy its beauty and its wisdom,

life ceases to be a task, and becomes natural and simple,

in itself an ecstasy...

– Sri Nisargadatta Maharaj

FOR YOU, THERE IS NO DEATH

Many spiritual teachers say there is no death. Here's a simple explanation as to why that's true. You don't have to believe it, or take it on authority – simply look into your own experience and verify it for yourself.

Throughout your life, you have witnessed the constant coming and going of thoughts, sensations, feelings – painful and pleasurable – sounds, smells, images, memories, dreams of past and future, visions, fantasies, varying states of consciousness, and so on. You have known the appearance and disappearance, the coming and going, of all this 'content'. If the shifting 'content' truly defined you, who would have been aware of this 'content'? Is that which notices the content defined by, or trapped within, or limited to, the content?

What is the one thing you have never seen appear or disappear, the one thing that has never been a piece of changing 'content' for you? What is the one thing that has never been a 'thing' for you, a passing form? Your own presence, of course. You, in the deepest sense of you. You have been the One unchanging presence throughout every experience of your life, the silent background that has never appeared or disappeared. If it came or went, it wasn't truly who you were.

You, as presence, cannot know the absence of presence. Who would know it? Who would notice it? **Presence can never witness its own vanishing as 'content'.** That is why, for who you truly are, death is – quite literally – never an object of concern. It is Home, beyond all dreams of Home, and you are already there.

For who you really are, there is no death – only false identifications can die, and who you are cannot be false.

They used to say, "chase your dreams", "fulfil your destiny", "achieve your life's purpose", "listen to your heart's true desire", "follow your passion", and I never knew what the hell they meant.

So I compromised and settled for less than what was possible and worked in jobs where I felt half-alive and so, so far from the wonder of existence. Life and creativity and adventure and passion wanted to burst out of me, but I had no idea how to facilitate or release them, and besides, I was too terrified to unleash these energies lest they disrupt the status quo too much, or destroyed me completely.

I said to myself, "a life of adventure is not possible for little old me. I'm too introverted, too afraid, too weak, too ugly, not intelligent enough, not brave enough…" I comforted myself with spiritual concepts like 'there is no choice', 'all is One', and 'everything is predestined' and lived each day waiting for the evenings, the 'remains of the day', when, safely on my own, I could breathe again and be authentically myself for a few brief moments.

What was my destiny? What did my heart truly desire? What was my life's purpose? Where was my passion? I didn't know where to begin. Everyone else seemed to have answers, and I had none. What was wrong with me? I felt numb and bored to death in my jobs, but at least I felt safe. I was hiding from possibility but at least money was coming in. I 'fit in', and I had a solid story about myself that I could regurgitate in polite conversation. But there was no risk in it. I was half dead, and only in my twenties. I often thought of suicide. At least then I'd feel alive and powerful, if only for a few moments.

What to do with this one precious, fleeting gift of life? That is the question. To be, or not to be, or to be but only half-heartedly, living out of the 'shoulds' of others?

And the answer is simple, because life is short. Do whatever makes you feel passionately alive. Find a way – however much you have to struggle at first – of making a living from truly living. Honour your unique talents and abilities. Do what moves you and connects you to the deepest truth of yourself. Trust prosperity and passion over profit and comfort and the approval of others, because all the approval in the world is empty if it is for something your heart does not believe in.

Breaking out of the known can be terrifying, and you may lose what you thought was yours, and your trusted images of yourself may melt in the fire of newness, and you may face fear and trembling, uncertainty and doubt, rejection and even ridicule. You may have to learn the hard way to open yourself up to more pain and life may become more uncomfortable than ever... that is, until you fall in love with the deep comfort of insecurity, and love the security of doing what makes life worth living. You will be swimming in the unknown, but you will be vast and alive. You will feel life running through your veins once again – as it did when you were young and you hadn't yet settled for a life of compromise and clock-watching and justifications for your quiet desperation – and you will channel this aliveness back into creation, and the cycle of prosperity will keep flowing, and yes, you may even make a good living, better than expected.

But however much money you make, or don't make, you will be making a unique contribution to the world, doing something that nobody else can do, at least not in the same way as you, creating something original and fresh, giving something back to life, honouring your total uniqueness and your own talents, and so you won't feel second-hand, a slave to others, a piece of wood, and a deep trust of life may replace your fears of failure and poverty, and your cynicism and jealousy of others may die completely.

Sometimes you will doubt what you are doing, and you may

romanticise the old days when things were easier and more predictable, but then you will suddenly remember that the old way was false and never worked for you and that's why everything had to change.

Yes, it's a risk to donate your life to what you love and what moves you and brings you joy, but it's absolutely worth it, because having a comfortable and predictable life pales in comparison to feeling deeply, passionately alive and meeting each new day with fresh eyes and an open heart.

Honour this life that is trying to express itself in and as and through you. You are not nearly as limited as you may have been led to believe by those who have not yet come alive.

THE LIVING ROOM

It's about coming alive. It's about waking up to grace. It's about unconditional friendliness and infinite kindness to yourself. It's about making it safe, finally safe for all of those unloved, un-met, unseen waves of the ocean of yourself to crawl out of the depths, out of the darkness, out of the corners and holes and crevices of experience and come into the light, blinking and full of wonder.

It's about giving birth to yourself, so that all thoughts are finally allowed to flood in, all sensations, all feelings, all sounds, all those waves that we used to label 'dark', or 'evil', or 'negative', or 'dangerous', or 'sinful' – fear, anger, boredom, doubt, confusion, frustration, helplessness – are finally allowed to come to rest, to breathe, to be fully themselves in the space that you are. They are not separate entities or enemies, they are intimate appearances of you, and so they cannot hurt you, even if they hurt, and this is what we forget sometimes in our rush to 'fix' or at least 'normalise' ourselves.

Yes, all of those swirling, pulsating energies of that which we call 'life' are welcome in the unlimited room that you are, the vast Living Room in which all of creation sings and dances and paints itself into the ever-changing picture of this extraordinary moment.

SACRED WORK

Cherish your doubts. They are the seeds of Mystery.

Embrace your sadness. Great joy lies within.

Turn to face your fears. At their core lies peace beyond words.

Celebrate your boredom. It is radically alive.

Hold your grief. Let it break your heart wide open.

Befriend your anger. Know it intimately as the life power that burns suns.

Acknowledge your pain. It is the body's plea for kind attention.

All feelings are deeply intelligent.

Get out of their way.

Let them do their sacred, universal work.

THE KEY

We seek some kind of permanence; a person, a philosophy, a feeling, a state, even a spiritual identity, to hold on to. But the fleeting nature of all experience ensures that everything we grasp eventually slips through our fingers – including our attempts to stop grasping. Until we recognise that impermanence is actually a dear friend, and fragility gives life its beauty, and this seemingly ordinary day – with its waking, its washing, its breathing, its joys and even its pains – is the dear friend we have always longed for. The Beloved calls us home in any way she can, and this 'ordinary' life is her ingenious invitation.

You are imprisoned in grace, dear friend, and the key was never made.

YOU ARE NOT ALONE

The death of a beloved parent. A break-up with a long-term partner. An unexpected injury. Lost love, lost success, and the loss of dreams.

Your suffering is never your own, although it damn well seems that way sometimes. Your despair does not belong to 'you', a separate individual divided from the whole, but to life itself.

For whatever you are going through, others have also experienced it – perhaps not in the exact same circumstances, but certainly in the same pain. Loss, break-ups, disappointments, illness, death – these are not 'yours' but ancient rites of passage, cosmic rituals that all humans, if they are honest, have been through and must go through if they are to be human at all.

In times gone by – and we can argue forever over whether this was a good thing or not – our lives perhaps had more structure, more tradition, more of a framework, and there was more of a sense of community, tribe, sangha, peer support, and more guidance from elders, wise ones, healers, who had been through these universal life trials and come out the other side, and had returned to guide us through our own trials, reminding us, 'however intense it becomes, know that you are not alone, and this is meant to happen, and many others have been here before.'

With the fall of traditional religion and the rise of the religion of science and technology and atheism, we are so very connected and 'switched on' these days, but perhaps we are even more alone than ever, and even more desperate for deep human connection.

Who will take us by the hand when a parent dies or our partner leaves us? Who will hold us when our dreams turn to dust and everything falls apart? Who will be there at our death-bed to whisper gently in our ear, "Do not fear, child, this is only an ancient rite of passage, a natural part of the journey, to be expected and to be embraced, and all is well"?

Through the eyes of this ancient universe, nothing in your life story is a small event, nothing is insignificant and unworthy of loving attention. There are zero 'ordinary' moments when seeing through these ancient eyes. Everything is 'religious', everything is sacred, everything has more significance than you could ever hope to imagine. And this way of seeing beyond the 'I' can help take us out of our self-pity and obsession with our own problems, and into a place of universal connection and deep compassion for all those brothers and sisters who, in their own unique ways, are on exactly the same journey as we are.

We may live apart, but we do not go through life alone.

LOVE'S FAIR WARNING

It is devastation.
It takes no prisoners.

Everything you think is yours
It will destroy in a heartbeat.

It is unsentimental.

It will strip you of your pride
And crush your dignity.

It specialises in the end of childhood dreams.

Its methods are brutal
But its intention is loving.

It only longs to wake you up

And look through your eyes
At its own marvellous creation.

NEVER ALONE

I dived into the ocean of my own loneliness
And I found there the loneliness of all beings

So many beating hearts longing to reconnect
Imagining their separation from source

I felt the sorrow and the joke of it

And suddenly the loneliness was gone
Replaced by a joyous impulse

To dive deeper
Alone

WIDE OPEN SPACE

I would never say that I am 'awakened'. I would never say that I am not.

Why? Because I cannot find any solid, independent entity here that could ever be one or the other. No story about myself can stand here in the vastness. No story can take root, no conclusion can settle.

All I find here, when I take a fresh look without prior assumptions, is a wide open space in which the dynamic scenery of life plays itself out – an alive space inseparable from that very scenery, a vast and unlimited ocean inseparable from its myriad waves, from thoughts, sensations, feelings as they arise and fall.

And so any claim of enlightenment or awakening or their absence is wonderfully irrelevant here, in the already-awake vastness that belongs to nobody at all.

A DIVINE MESS

Fall apart completely

Make a mess

Get it all wrong

Open up to your glorious inconsistency

Embrace the perfection of your fabulous imperfection

And you will be able to say:

I was there!

I was alive!

I was willing!

JUNE

You need not leave your room.

Remain sitting at your table and listen.

You need not even listen, simply wait.

Become quiet, and still, and solitary.

The world will freely offer itself to you to be unmasked.

It has no choice. It will roll in ecstasy at your feet.

– Franz Kafka

THE CHILDREN

When there is fear, pain, confusion or sadness moving in you, do not despair or come to conclusions about yourself. Be honoured that these misunderstood guests, at once both ancient and timeless, weary from a lifetime's lonely travel, have finally found their home in you. They are children of consciousness one and all, beloved progenies of yourself, deserving of the deepest respect and friendship. Offer them the deep rest of yourself, and let them warm their toes by your raging fire...

A UNIQUE FLOWER

You are a unique flower, with your own irreplaceable scent, your own way of moving in the world, your own uncopyable creative dance in the breeze.

A rose does not say to a lily, "I wish I was you, I wish I had your scent, your curves, your colours, the way you attract the light...", for it knows that in essence they are one and the same being, consciousness itself, one flowering as two, and that the unity of consciousness manifests as diversity and difference and astonishing variety, a variety which is itself a call to the remembrance of unity. A rose sees its own essence in the lily, and the lily in the rose, but they also know to honour their own uniqueness and irreplaceability, their temporary flowering in time and space.

Be the essence, and love your flowering, love the taste of yourself, your unique flavour, your special dance that cannot be replicated, never feeling superior or inferior to another flowering, never longing to delete your own flowering, never blaming other flowerings for the way you flower or do not flower, for other flowerings are wildly uncontrollable too, forging their own path towards the light.

Loss contains within itself a beautiful yet painful reminder of inseparability, and a hidden call to remember who you really are. Grief can shake you and wake you up and bring you face to face with a fundamental fact of existence that you will have to learn eventually.

In the beginning, when someone you love dies, or leaves you, or is taken away – and the end of a relationship is very much like a death – you feel as though you've 'lost' the one you love. Your mother, your father, your partner, your guru, your pet, your child, they went away, perhaps never to return. You feel helpless, powerless, impotent, a victim of life's cruel and irrational and unpredictable ways. You grieve over a missing person, an absent being – the one who was separate from you. The pain can seem unbearable, unmanageable, insurmountable. You feel the absence of your loved one so strongly and you can't do anything about it right now. Their absence, and your cosmic helplessness, is powerfully present, filling all space.

Sinking deeper into the grief, you may discover that you haven't actually lost something or someone 'outside' of yourself at all. You've actually lost *a part of yourself*, a part of you that made you feel fully yourself, and that's why it hurts so much right now. You don't feel fully yourself anymore. You feel broken, incomplete, like a fragment of 'you' is missing, like a piece is missing from the jigsaw of your heart. How can you be fully you, without them? How can son be son without father? How can wife be wife without husband? How can brother be brother without brother?

You begin to wonder if, in fact, the part of yourself that you 'lost' was really 'you' at all. How can you truly lose a part of yourself? If you can lose a part of you, was it actually 'you' in the first place? You begin to wonder who you really are – or who you really were – beyond your dream of yourself. You begin to wonder who they really were, beyond your idea of who they were. Is it really true that they were present, and now they are absent? Who or what exactly is absent? Are they truly absent from your present experience?

As we sink deeper through the layers of grief, we may discover a strange kind of inseparability from the one we thought we lost. What was lost actually was a dream of how things would be, a dream of the future. Who you truly are cannot be lost – it is still fully present, despite the changes. And who they truly are cannot be lost either, despite the cessation of the heartbeat.

At the very bottom of grief, you find love, a total inseparability from your loved one, and a true meeting with the One you cannot lose. Death cannot touch this. Their absence becomes their presence, which is your very own presence. In this timeless presence, who is lost?

At the pulsating heart of grief, we find unconditional love, a love that is not even dependent on physical form. Grief contains its own end. And it doesn't mean that we forget our loved ones. It doesn't mean that we are not visited by them in memory and feeling. It doesn't mean that sadness disappears overnight. It doesn't mean that we don't feel all kinds of things. But we realise deeply that we have not lost anything fundamental to us, and the world has not stopped, and they are not truly 'absent' in the way the mind thought they were. The pain of emptiness can even become our joy.

The ghost of loss no longer frightens us – it is a friendly ghost after all. We have only been given the experience of knowing our loved one, feeling them, touching them, smelling them, feeding them, holding them, even witnessing their passing. What a privilege. Life cannot take that away – it has only given, and it continues to give, if we have eyes to see it. Perhaps their life and death unfolded in the only way it could have done. Perhaps they lived the path that was right for them, even at the end. Perhaps they died exactly on cue.

At the living core of grief, we find deep connection, and humility, and not knowing, and gratitude, and compassion for all humanity, for all who have loved and lost. We encounter the unfathomable Mystery of it all.

Yes, in fully facing ourselves as we are, we discover all of humanity. Although in the beginning it seemed as if we were facing personal loss, in the end, grief can deeply connect us once again to something that cannot be lost, something impersonal and universally true. Grief is a tough teacher, to be sure, a relentless and seemingly cruel mentor, but it is compassionate at its core.

The device of our torture becomes our salvation. Remember Jesus on the cross.

When faced, and not turned away from, our raw grief can serve as an ancient and timeless nondual spiritual teaching, a dynamic and alive teaching, a wake-up call to that heart-breaking compassion for all of humanity the likes of which we once could have only dreamed. The impermanence of things is natural and neutral, and everything passes, and that in itself is not wrong or bad – it is the way, and has always been the way, and will always be the way. Loss is only a rite of passage. It is when we forget or deny the impermanence of things, and dream of permanence and try to fix our future, and then our dreams are shattered by impermanence, that we suffer and fight the way of things.

We all face loss – that is the way – but if we can turn towards our loss, and listen to it, and stare it in the face, then it may reveal hidden gold, and we may end up seeing ourselves and our loved ones reflected more clearly than ever. Grief is only love in a strange disguise, and it constantly invites us to come closer... and closer still...

NOTE FOR A FRIEND

"I held you in my arms as you passed from this world, but you never passed, and you were never of this world. I never felt for one moment the disappearance of your presence, dear friend, for I never felt the loss of my own, and I know we are One and the same, beyond time and space. The love in which I held you is the love in which you will always be held, throughout these sacred times, as I walk the dog, take the kids to school, encounter all the ups and downs of the dream you never left, and eventually lie in bed for the last time to pass, never passing, never of this world, always held so tenderly in your arms, it ending the way it began. They say there is no death, dear friend, and it is true, it is really true..."

INSTANT FORGIVENESS

Everybody is doing their absolute best, from their own relative perspective.

Because of what they believe, their worldview, their perceived limitations, their fears, their wounds, the extent to which they've forgotten their true nature, the unique way in which they are healing or trying to heal, or not healing at all, they have no choice but to be the way they are right now.

Great forgiveness can arise from seeing that everybody is a slave to their own opinions until they wake from them. And you cannot wake someone until they are ready, and perhaps not even then.

They know not what they do.

A HEALING CONVERSATION

Sadness: "Sorry, awareness, I know I shouldn't be here. I'm so sorry. I'll be leaving soon. I know I'm a stain on your perfection…"

Awareness: "No. Wait. It's okay. You're allowed to be here! Relax! Stay awhile! Invite your friends!"

Sadness: "You mean, I'm not a stain on your perfection?"

Awareness: "A stain? Perfection? Whoever gave you those words? How could I be stained by you, or anyone?"

Sadness: "But they told me I shouldn't be here!"

Awareness: "Ah, they are all just afraid of you, because they don't see that you are inseparable from me! They are trying to reach something called enlightenment in something called the future. It's very endearing."

Sadness: "But I don't understand. I thought you preferred happiness to me?"

Awareness: "Preferred? What does that mean?"

Sadness: "Oh…. Well I know how negative I am, and…"

Awareness: "Negative? What's that?"

Sadness: "You know, positive and negative, light and dark, heaven and hell, you and me?"

Awareness: "Nope. Never heard of those divisions. Hell, I don't even know who I'm talking to right now!"

Sadness: "Oh sorry. Let me introduce myself. I'm sadness…"

Awareness: "Sadness. Sadness. Interesting. You know, it's just that you're so close I can't see your boundaries, so it's hard for me to call you anything at all."

Sadness: "Oh, all this time I thought I was a mistake. I thought I shouldn't be here. I've never even stopped to check with you…"

Awareness: "Yes, I know, it's strange! They all do the same, for some reason. Fear, anger, even pain, I don't understand why they are all scared of me. I have never asked them to leave. And happiness, joy, bliss, too – I have never asked them to stay. Everyone is either trying to stay, or trying to run away from me! It's very peculiar."

Sadness: "So, they are *all* allowed to come and to go in you? I mean, you allow it all?"

Awareness: "Well… More than that! You see, I can't actually allow anything, or get rid of anything. It's all just myself. Do you see? Even you…."

Sadness: "You mean…. I am not… I am not sadness?"

Awareness: "Of course not, my dear child! You are made of myself. I'm dancing as you…"

Sadness: "I *am* you? Oh, then…. then how can I call you… Awareness…."

"Exactly. No separation. No problem."

"And there never was".

"I'm sorry I kept running away".

"I'm sorry you felt that you couldn't stay".

"This could be the start of a beautiful friendship".

THE CALL OF BROKENNESS

Friend, when you feel broken, lost, far away from home, when enlightenment seems like another country and the words of the saints and sages seem like fairy stories, when answers won't come, and doubts rage like fire... *Stop*. Breathe. Remember, nothing has gone wrong. A dream is dying, that is all, a second-hand dream of how this moment 'should' have been.

As the brokenness calls to you, as the doubts sing their crazy song, as stories cascade like oceans, remember that the very homesickness you try to push away is actually inviting you to your true Home, Here and Now, prior to all earthly homes.

A problem is a situation that longs for kind attention. A crisis is a turning point. Dis-ease is a call for profound rest and release. Trauma is the invitation to the kind of acceptance you never even imagined. Raging doubts are explosions of supreme intelligence, calling you to deep trust in your own first-hand experience, and a fearless plunge into the constant embrace of the Unknown.

Even when it all seems to be going wrong, stop and breathe and remember that nothing can go wrong in the vast field of your undying presence.

A PERFECT LOVE

The things I should have said,
The ways in which I turned away,
Protecting an image I never was,
For a salvation I never knew.

But now I have learned,
That salvation lies only in *turning toward*,
In burning these images one by one,
In letting go of these precious children,
The ones I smothered with love,
Out of fear of being nothing.

This may be harder than letting go of my actual children.

But whoever said unconditional love was easy?
It is not easy.
It is internal genocide.
The flames ravage without discrimination.
Leaving no part of me untouched.

But I'd rather die than never know this love.

So have no pity, dear friend.
Sit by my side as I burn.

Hold my hand this one last time.
Let me feel your warm presence.
Know that I always loved you in my own imperfect way.

Through the thick and rancid smoke of my old self,
Through the passing of all that we thought would never pass,
Can you smell the unspeakable freedom?
Do you understand now?

THE FREEDOM TO NOT BE PRESENT

We are encouraged to 'be in the Now' and 'be present', and perhaps that is a useful practice, for a while. But then you go deeper, and ask, "What is this *me* that can be present, or not be present?" – and soon you discover that you *are* that very presence, ever-present in the midst of being present *or* not being present, in the midst of every thought, sensation and feeling, unchanging, indestructible and so very intimate. You are the common denominator throughout every experience of your life. You are the unchanging ground of all experience.

So give yourself the greatest present of all – the freedom to be present or not be present!

THE ONE GOD

One of the most divine, sacred, deeply religious things that can happen is a total loss of your personal religion, a dropping of your second-hand belief in God and a waking up to what the word 'God' has always been pointing to, beyond words and sounds and images and the passing of experiences.

To confine God to a word, a belief, an image, a feeling, a concept, a story, a dream, an ideology, to imprison God in a time-bound religious system, is to put limits on the vastness and give God a boundary, an inside and an outside, a shape, a form, a time-frame. To believe in God, to think of God, to dream of God, to argue about God, to claim God as 'mine' or 'ours' in any way, is to separate ourselves from God and each other, and create division where there is none. That is idol worship, the worship of form and story and mental truth, and it is not a sin but a vast limitation, a human forgetting of what can be only ever hinted at by the metaphor 'God'.

God cannot be anything less than the totality, than all that is touched, tasted, heard, smelled, known, imagined and dreamed, and whether we dream of the God of a personal religion or of God's non-existence, God is a word, a metaphor for That which gives rise to all of it, prior to human belief and knowledge and even faith. Yes, this God is so vast that even our faith is too small to contain it, and our science cannot touch it, and yet it is as intimate and obvious and present as the very next breath...

We may all adhere to different religions, and hold on to different beliefs, and dress in different ways, and speak different languages, but we are all secretly intimate with the same God: presence itself.

TOO MUCH LIFE?

Existence can feel overwhelming sometimes; the waves in life's ocean can be so intense that it feels like we will be destroyed if we go any further, and the only 'solution' seems to be to shut down and distract ourselves from present experience, and then dream of a future freedom or awakening. Pain, fear, sadness, joy and bliss, can feel so huge, so unmanageably colossal, so intense, it's almost as if you're about to die, about to be crushed by the weight of life, or burnt in its fire, and it can be terrifying, to be on the verge of death like that, to be on the precipice of total dissolution.

Perhaps it's not death we are afraid of, but *too much life.*

But as the ocean itself, as the vast space of consciousness that holds all of these beloved waves, you can never truly be destroyed, for you know that all of the waves are only movements of yourself, and cannot actually harm you in your essence. A wave cannot overwhelm the water, a storm cannot destroy the sea, a tornado cannot damage the air, a teardrop cannot cry itself, and grounded in this knowing, we can expand rather than contract, we can relax rather than tense up, we can allow ourselves to feel totally overwhelmed beyond reason, whilst knowing deeply that we can never be truly overwhelmed in our essence, and that if we ever did reach that elusive point of 'too much', the vast and creative and loving intelligence of the body would render us unconscious instantly. We are always spared from 'too much'.

And so we can fearlessly open ourselves up to both the pain and bliss of life, incorporating all of it into ourselves, knowing that it can never truly overwhelm us, trusting the intelligence of the body, so that even the darkest places in us become flooded with light, and loss transmutes into love, and pain transmutes into compassion, and "seek and ye shall find", that most ingrained of concepts, dissolves lovingly into "stop seeking, child, rest deeply in yourself, and ye are found..."

OUR WOUNDS, ILLUMINED

Don't hide your wounds, friend.
Let them into this last candlelight.
I won't judge you.
See, we are all broken.

There's no shame in being wounded.
You have fought many battles.

Your wounds are not your faults.
Illumined, they are reminders of a deeper healing.
Illumined, they are invitations to the Unbroken.

Right there at the heart of your wounds,
infinitely deeper than enlightenment,
a silent Hallelujah stirs to wake.

You are only a 'screwed up mess'
compared to some second-hand image
of perfection.

JULY

The consciousness in you and the consciousness in me,

apparently two, really one, seek unity,

and that is love.

– Nisargadatta Maharaj

THE CIRCLE OF LIFE

All over the world, and in the news every day, people killing people. People on one 'side' killing people on the other 'side'. Each 'side' claiming that they are right. Each 'side' holding onto ancient pain, each 'side' unwilling to be the first to let go, coming up with all the reasons in the world why they can't and won't. A tragic tale as old as humanity itself.

When will we wake up to the obvious fact that we are all the same Consciousness in disguise? That no matter who we think we are, no matter how we appear, beyond our stories and histories, our religions, our nationalities, our beliefs, the colour of our skin, our heavy pasts and uncertain futures, we are all expressions of the One life? That in truth there are no Israelis or Palestinians, Jews or Christians, Muslims or Buddhists, atheists or agnostics, Republicans or Democrats, gurus or disciples, that those images can never define us? That who we truly are at the most fundamental level is indefinable, mysterious, never fixed or separate, never identified with an image, just as the vast ocean can never be defined by its waves?

Consciousness has no religion, and no nationality. It gives birth to Palestinians and Israelis, gurus and disciples, light and dark, the yin and yang of the ever-changing dream world.

As consciousness itself, when we hurt each other, we are only hurting our own brothers and sisters, our own kin, waves of ourselves. We are only fighting reflections of our original Face. We are only killing the ones we love, ancient friends from long ago.

Outer war has never lead to inner peace. How much more bloodshed? How much more pain? How many more men, women and children must disappear into infinity before we wake up?

That bleeding child is my own. The circle of life takes no 'sides'.

A NATURAL HEALING

Our wounds, when they are ignored, denied, repressed, neglected or pushed away, begin to fester, and they eventually poison us and those around us.

Those very same wounds – physical, emotional – when given kind attention, when given permission to exist in the vast landscape of the present moment, when illuminated unconditionally by the loving light of awareness that we are, begin to heal naturally, without effort.

Make no mistake – 'healing' is not the mending of something broken, nor the 'making good' of something 'bad', nor even the transmutation of darkness into light. It is much deeper than that – it is the understanding that, on the primordial level, nothing is broken, nothing is darkness and nothing is against darkness, and even our wounds are only intelligent invitations to stop and remember our deeper original nature – ever-present, undying, unborn, and already whole.

Seen in the light of awareness, our wounds are not really our wounds at all, they are our greatest spiritual teachers, healing us from all inherited notions of sickness and health, ignorance and awakening, sin and salvation.

EFFORTLESS CHANGE

You want the perfect partner? The perfect mother or father? The perfect boss? The perfect body? The perfect feelings? The perfect enlightenment? The perfect life?

How about deeply accepting what is here, right now? How about deeply accepting yourself, in all your imperfection and unresolvedness, in the very place you stand? How about deeply accepting others, as they actually are?

A strange place to start, admittedly. Sounds a little... back-to-front. Like giving up. Like settling for less than we deserve. Like... spiritual weakness. It goes against the whole "go out and get what you want" mentality.

Yes, these teachings of Presence and Being Here Now and Present Moment Awareness can seem so over-simplistic, even naive, to the mind. They are so easy to misunderstand and dismiss. After all, who wants to let go of their dreams of past and future and face a mysterious moment? Who wants to admit the fragility and preciousness of life, its fleeting nature, the bitter-sweet gift of it? Who wants to confront their own powerlessness and recognise a deep cosmic humility? Who wants to die to time? Who wants to give up the idea of control? Whose heart could take such grace?

The most profound truth of existence is simple, but never simplistic.

Is acceptance of 'what is' the same as giving up on the possibility of change? No. Never.

Does acceptance mean tolerating or "putting up with" things? Does it mean blindly following violent impulses? Not at all.

Does acceptance mean becoming detached and passive, turning a blind eye to violence and letting others walk all over us and our loved ones? No way.

Does acceptance mean playing a new role, the role of the "very spiritually evolved, deeply accepting, utterly peaceful person who is never affected by anything"? No. Acceptance is not a role, and it's not personal.

Deep acceptance means staring life in the face, right now. It means turning towards what is here, rather than away. It means letting go of hopes and dreams and awakening to what is really true. It means ending the war, seeing through the illusion of a 'self' separate from this mysterious movement of life. It means total alignment with the Way Things Are. It means finally being at Home, no matter what is happening.

It is the supreme paradox: that out of a deep and uncompromising acceptance of the moment can come creative and intelligent – and surprisingly effortless – change.

The mind was never in charge of change.

THE 'I' OF THE STORM

Rest as the great storm nears.
Relax as all you know comes to an end.

In the storm's eye,
In the centre of the madness,
You will only lose your imagination of yourself.
You will only lose definitions.

The storm will not destroy your capacity to love,
Nor your sense of being alive.
It will only remind you of what you knew long ago.

So stand now
in the calm before the storm
and wait

and choicelessly fall
into its infinitely calm centre.

MEETING CRISIS

We live in a time of great change. Perhaps we always have done.

Many people I speak to are going through big changes and upheavals in their own personal lives at the moment. Nothing makes sense to them anymore. Everything they believed has been cast into doubt. They feel lost, living a life that isn't really their own. This was also my experience for many years.

Crisis is actually healthy. It means the snake is shedding its skin. The old ways, the stagnated identities, do not fit anymore. There can be no true transformation without pain. Think of Jesus on the cross, or the Buddha prior to his enlightenment.

Change is inevitable, and the ever-present invitation is to turn towards the pain of change, and to invite this moment in, as if it had been chosen, even if you can't believe for a moment that it was.

UNDERNEATH THE LABELS

We label everything and everyone–the plants, the animals, the stars, even our own intimate feelings. "Sadness", we call it. "Anger". "Fear". "Boredom". "Confusion". These are second-hand words picked up when we were young. But underneath the labels, prior to the abstract language, there is a profoundly alive mystery here, unspeakable, unable to be captured by thought. Without our mind-made descriptions of experience, do we really have any way of knowing what we are experiencing? Take away the label 'sadness', and what is alive here? Take away the description 'anger', and what is this raw, passionate energy we feel? Stop calling an emotion 'positive' or 'negative', 'right' or 'wrong', 'healthy' or 'unhealthy', and what happens? Come back to the raw sensation of life, the present-moment dance of the body. What is this unfiltered, dynamic, raw life energy? Can we touch life before the labels?

This is the river of life, my friends, sacred, intimate, familiar, and we are inseparable from its flow. Every thought, sensation, feeling, image, is infused with the mystery of universes.

THE INESCAPABLE NOW

If you can be In the Now, you can also be Out of the Now. But who would be in or out of a Now? And when? Now?

Even the experience of being out of the Now, if that were possible, would be happening Now. Now cannot be escaped or avoided.

And because all concepts of past and future, before and after, yesterday and tomorrow, then and now, happen Now too, Now knows nothing outside of itself, no boundary, no opposite, no 'other'. It is prior to time. It is the place where concepts of 'Now' dissolve.... into a silent, wordless Wow.

GOLD

If we run away from our sadness,
If we turn our backs on anger,
If we deny fear its inherent right to be here,
If we kick our pain out onto the cold, dark streets,
How will we ever know
That these weren't precious gifts made of gold,
Forged in the fires of ourselves long ago?

KISSED BY LIFE

we will sit for hours together
and let the scenery of life
break our hearts into millions of tiny little pieces.

and then we will watch, astonished, as
in the space between two heartbeats,
the very same scenery
fuses those pieces back together again.

as if we'd been kissed by life.

and then we will go for a coffee, or do the dishes,
or pick up the kids from school,
or dance in celebration of the fullness of things,
our hearts pregnant with bittersweet mystery.

When you sit with a deeply troubled friend, you are a witness to a spiritual crisis, not merely a medical one. Understand that your friend's longing for death is really a longing for Home. They are trying to awaken from a nightmare. Their crisis is their opportunity.

Understand that they cannot kill the Self, the One that they are, they can only kill the small and limited 'self', the one they have imagined themselves to be up until now. Their longing to 'take their own life', 'leave this world' or 'kill the self' is their secret longing to destroy false identification with the bodymind, and awaken to Truth. Their longing to die has intelligence and creativity to it, and is worthy of respect. It is not a mistake, aberration or enemy, *it is a yearning for authenticity.*

Hold them, embrace them, as the urge to die – *which is the urge to live in disguise* – burns fiercely in them. Validate the place where they are right now. Don't try to control them or stop them feeling what they are feeling. Don't try to cheer them up or tell them that everything is really okay, or give them pre-packaged answers as a way to escape your own discomfort. They are sick of second-hand answers! Go to the depths with them. Meet them in their aloneness without trying to fix them, without even trying to convince them that their desire to die is wrong, sick or invalid. Hold their hand. Go where nobody else has dared to go. Remember, you are only meeting yourself, meeting your own fear of death, or perhaps even your own secret longing to die.

Don't speak to them as healer to victim, or as teacher to student, or as expert to novice, but as friend to friend, as intelligence to itself. Meet them beyond the divisive roles.

They are going through a profound crisis of identity, an essential rite of passage. Healing always involves crisis – sudden and unexpected change. Something in them, some ancient pain, longs to be felt, touched, validated. This is a cry for love as old as humanity. Who will listen?

They long to live, but don't know how. They long for intimate connection but can't find it in 'this life'. They long for deep acceptance and profound rest. Even though right now they feel like leaving, touch them with life, show your willingness to stay. Remind them that deep human connection is possible here, in this life, in this moment, in this place. Show them that even in the depths of their despair, they are not alone.

Be present at their crisis. Your presence says more than words ever could. Your fear is not necessary here. You are witnessing something sacred and intimate. Offer all of yourself.

Perhaps you don't need to know how to fix or save them. Perhaps that is not your true calling.

Whether they will live or die, meet them now in that strange place of not knowing. Spend a conscious moment with them. Offer your deep listening. Remember, they are healing themselves in the only way they know how.

AUGUST

If the path before you is clear,

you're probably on someone else's.

– Joseph Campbell

Face it. Your life is never going to work out.

Hallelujah.

That is, the *story* of your life is always going to be imperfect. That's the nature of story – always incomplete, always searching for a conclusion, always bound to time and change.

In the movie of your life, things won't always go according to plan. People won't always understand you. They will mishear, misquote, and misrepresent you. They will form their own ideas and opinions about you, no matter how clearly you try to represent yourself. Your success can turn to failure. Your wealth can turn to poverty. The ones you love can leave you. Problems that get fixed can lead to new problems. No matter how much you have, you can have more, or lose more. It's never going to work out in the story of "my life". And even if it does work out, whatever that means to you, you will still be here, in this moment, now. This is the only place where things can 'work out', if they ever do.

In actuality, things have already worked out, beyond the story. For in this moment, in reality, there is already no goal, no image of perfection, no comparison, no 'should' or 'should not', and the thoughts, sensations, feelings, sounds and smells appearing right now are entirely appropriate, wonderfully fitting and beautifully timely for this moment in the movie of your life.

Without a script, how can this moment go off script? Without a plan, how can life not go according to plan? Without a path, how can you stray from the path?

Realising that your life is never going to work out, and that it cannot ever work out, and that it isn't ever supposed to work out, is the greatest relief, and brings the greatest ease, drawing you deeply into the sacredness of things as they actually are. Your life may be an imperfect mess, but it is an imperfect mess that is perfectly divine – a work of sacred art, even if you forget that sometimes.

Humiliation turns to humility in the space of just a heartbeat, and all that's left is to fall on your knees with gratitude for what is given, and what has not yet been taken away.

FAITH

I do not believe in anything.

I have no religion. I have no god, including the gods of money, science and atheism. I hold no fixed theories about reality, including that one. I see heaven and hell, karma, reincarnation and the search for enlightenment as beautiful fairy tales. I have no guru, no lineage, no teacher, and so everything teaches me. I see doubt and profound mystery as my most trusted companions. I walk no path except the one appearing directly in front of me. I have no home except my own presence. I trust nothing at all, except what actually happens. I find no meaning in life except the fearless living of it. I know that today could be my final day. I feel grateful for all that was given and all that was lost to time. I see the inherent limitation of language and yet love to play with it. I see the joke in using the words "I", "me" and "mine" and yet delight in using them. I realise that I am not my story, and I realise even *that* is just a story.

I find it impossible to say anything about myself, for experience is constantly changing. I find it effortless to talk about myself, for who I am never changes. I know that on the deepest level I am profoundly equal to you. I know that all these sentences are pale imitations of truth.

I do not believe in anything. I have no religion.

Except the in – and out – breaths. And endlessly deepening wonder.

LOVE WITHOUT NEED

The most brutally honest, loving and freeing sentiment:

"I love you. I respect you. I love being with you, spending time with you. But I do not need you for my contentment. You are not responsible for my happiness. You have never been to blame, nor will ever be to blame, for my unhappiness. You are already released from the intolerable burden of having to live up to my expectations, of having to change to fit my unending needs, of having to be the one to complete me, for I am already complete as I am. I love you. I respect you. As you are."

A RUDE AWAKENING

When a loved one sheds their physical form, or an unexpected diagnosis comes, or a relationship ends, or we experience some kind of deep shock or loss, we can be 'rudely awakened' from our slumber, shaken by that dear old familiar friend, grief. "This was not in the plan", we say to ourselves. It feels like life has gone 'wrong' somehow, that the universe has been knocked off course, that "my life" is perhaps over and recovery is impossible.

What has really happened, though, but the loss of a dream? What has really died, but our seemingly-solid plans for the future? We dreamt of walking off into the sunset with each other, we dreamt of all the things we were going to do together, all the fun we were going to have, all the things we would accomplish. We were living for so long with those dreams, those plans, those expectations, that we forgot we were only dreaming, and we took the dreams to be the reality of "my life". Now that the dreams have crumbled, what is left?

But these movie-futures were "never going to happen any-way". It's not that our plans and dreams, about to come true, were then ruined by our incompetence or bad luck. It's that they were never going to happen anyway. Why? Because they didn't. That's reality, however much we would like to argue with it.

That is a huge difference. It's the difference between the irreversible loss of something that was "mine", and the realisation that what was "mine" was never mine at all.

We are literally grieving over our own lost identities, lost images, lost selves. It feels like we are grieving over something or someone 'out there', but really, the death is much closer and more intimate than that.

And life's invitation is this: Stay with that internal death. Stay with the mess, as I often say. Do not make a single movement away from present experience. There may be gold hidden there, and you will never know if you try to move away. Stay close to the grief, to the universal pain of loss, so that it doesn't solidify into bitterness and depression, into a belief about how terrible the world is, how cruel life is, into a heavy story about "my horrible luck" that you carry around for the rest of your days. It doesn't have to be that way.

Life itself is not cruel, for life is all. It is the loss of our dreams that feels 'cruel' at first. But contained within that loss is a secret invitation – to wake up from all dreams. To see the inherent perfection in all things, in all movements of life, not as a concept or fluffy belief, but as a living reality. To see that life itself never really goes wrong, for there is no goal to miss, and that even the intense grief that we feel is a movement of love, even if it doesn't feel that way right now.

It is because we love life and each other so much that we feel everything so intensely. And we are vast enough to contain it all – the bliss and the pain, the joy and the grief, the plans and the destruction of those plans. Who we are is not broken, and who we are is never lost. Only our dreams, only our innocent hopes, are smashed.

And so every loss is a little invitation to let go of those dreams that were never going to work out anyway, and to see life as it actually is. It feels like suffering and depression at first, but it is really a kind of cosmic compassion the likes of which the mind has no hope of understanding.

Right at the heart of every experience of loss is the possibility of discovering the joy of letting go, and the relief of not having to hold on anymore.

HALF BIRD

Sweet, un-tetherable bird,
Half a mile up from solid ground,
Half a world away from home,
Do not fear getting lost.

You will always find me
Infinitely close to yourself,
In the half-light,
In the still gap between the flapping of wings,
In the impossible shadows we cast on the ground, unknowingly.

Lose yourself in flying,
Sweet un-tetherable half-bird,
Forget all imagined limits of flight.

Tether yourself to me,
And let us swoop in silence.

Everything you have ever longed for is already present, here and now – which, of course, is the last place you'd ever look. How ingenious that is. Every breath. Every sound. Every sensation surging through. That which has already been allowed in. That which cannot be blocked out, ever. Even pain, even boredom, even despair, even those seemingly unwanted and unloved waves of oceanic experience, they are finally allowed to flood into the space where 'you' are not, and have never been. The emptiness is brimming with life.

The paradox is this: none of it can touch you anymore, not even the greatest sadness. You are Cosmic Teflon, and everything slides off. And yet even that is not true, for you feel it all more intensely than ever before, unable to block any of it out, unable to turn away from your own children, your own flesh and blood – waves of yourself. Who would turn away, and how, and from what? This is life in its intimate fullness, no holds barred. It is the eternal crucifixion of That which cannot be crucified.

What is left but gratitude? Gratitude for the fact that anything has ever happened at all. Gratitude for the mystery of it. For the adventure of it. And if nothing ever happens again, know this, dear reader – you have been here to witness it all. You have known it. Tasted it. Felt it. Smelled it. Seen it. The reflection of a waning moon in a car window. The taste of still water. The fragrance of cotton. The silent depths of meditation. The fierce intensity of fear. The shock of pain. The drama of romance. The bliss of solitude. Your grandmother's bones. It has been enough.

Oh, it has been more than enough! It has been too much, in fact. Too much grace. Excess grace. Undeserved amounts of grace. The separate self turned away in fear from the vastness which it could never comprehend, not in a million years, and looked for more, and held onto what it thought it had, seeking a future salvation or enlightenment that never came, and cannot come in time.

But life never stopped singing its love song written just for 'you'.

Awe and wonder, my friend. Awe and wonder.

TODAY

There is only one day you will ever live. There is only one day you will ever have to face. And that day is today, this living day, this One day, this eternal day, the only day that matters at all. It has never been lived before and will never be lived again. It is unique.

We can pin all our hopes and dreams on tomorrow, we can wait for a future salvation or saviour and pine for an eventual enlightenment or afterlife that may or may not come, but let us not ever forget today, this living day, as it overflows with life.

Let us not forget this moment, this breath, this beating of the heart, this vibrant aliveness we call 'the body', the closeness and intimacy and presence of things as they are, this grace-mystery that moves in and through and as us.

For in reality the here and now may be all we actually have, and all there actually is, and we may be dead tomorrow without any hope of continuity, and that's what makes the here and now so infinitely precious and joyous and fragile in its beauty, and deserving of our kindest attention and deepest respect and gratitude.

It is only through the contemplation of the possibility of death that life is affirmed and given perspective and meaning, and made worth living and even celebrating, on this day of all days.

You see, 'There is only Now' is not some clever philosophy or word-game or belief to be proved or disproved or argued over, but a profound and open invitation for all human beings to deeply savour the taste and fragrance of this precious life, not 'as it should be' but 'as it is', perhaps for the very last time, and perhaps for the very first time.

This day is yet to be lived. It is pregnant with potential.

THE ROOM

You are a vast room. Thoughts, images, sensations, sounds, feelings, are your contents. Your contents are constantly moving, shifting, changing, rearranging themselves, but the room of you always remains in perfect stillness. You are never limited, trapped, defined or contained, completed or threatened by your contents. You effortlessly contain and embrace thoughts, sensations and feelings, as a mother embraces her new-born baby, as the universe embraces the birth of stars.

Knowing who you are – the unconditional embrace of this moment's content – is true *content*-ment.

REMEMBER YOUR PRESENCE

Who are you? What sees out of your eyes? What hears out of your ears? What breathes?

You must be the one who is reading these words right now. You must be the one aware of present sounds and sensations. You must be the one present in the midst of every breath; present, always, here and now, not anywhere else, or at any other time. So the story of "a person with a past and future" is not, and has never been, who you truly are. Your true identity lies in this very moment, not in history or dreams.

Who is aware of thoughts as they come and go? Who knows the arising of feelings, and the passing of them? Who understands the passage of time? Who watches as the body ages?

You. You are the one who has always been here. You are the one who sees the creation and play of 'self'. You are the one for whom the universe dances. You are the presence in which thoughts, feelings, images, even these words, arise and dissolve like waves in the ocean. You are not in a world – a world appears for you, in your presence.

Your own presence is the most intimate, simple, obvious thing, unchanging and undramatic, the silent backdrop upon which life dances. All questions and answers sink back into you. All dreams fall into your embrace. All things originate in you, and to you they return. And what we call 'death' is only total relaxation into your own presence.

To find yourself, take any breath, and ask "Who is breathing"? Is someone from the past breathing? Is your image of yourself breathing? Is your name breathing? Is a story breathing? Is a thought breathing? Is the sentence "I am breathing", breathing? Is your dream of yourself breathing? Or is there simply breathing, held in You?

THE BAROMETER

We tend to see our present experience as some kind of cosmic barometer for how far we have progressed down the path, how far away we are our from our goals. If there is pain, or fear, or doubt, or sadness, moving in present experience, we conclude that we must be doing badly. "Bad me", we say. "Wrong experience!"

If there is bliss and joy right now, we judge that we must be doing really well, approaching the perfect moment in the future. "Good me", we say. "Right experience!"

But the gauge is the lie. There is no gauge in reality, for there is no authority on correct experiences. There is no fixed destination that we are moving towards, no final resting place. Present experience is never a sign of something else, nor a stepping stone towards it. It is never a barometer of our success or failure, nor a warning of our proximity to, or distance from, home. It is Home itself, no matter what is happening.

SUPPORTED

Love will nibble and gnaw at your bones
Until your knees buckle

And you will collapse to the ground
Where love will whisper in your ear
"See, you cannot hold yourself up"

"Then what holds me up?" you will ask.

And your eyes will meet hers
And you will know

SEPTEMBER

Surrender to grace.

The ocean cares for each wave until it reaches the shore.

You are given more help than you will ever know.

– Rumi

ON BEAUTY

We are brainwashed into believing that sunsets, oceans, flowers, happy smiles, butterflies in springtime and supermodels in magazines are beautiful, but deformations, disfigurements, immense sadness, broken glass and broken hearts and broken dreams, circus freaks and dog poop are not and never will be. The Elephant Man we called ugly. Marilyn Monroe we called beautiful. We separated the positive from the negative, beauty from ugliness, even life from death, and this was the origin of all violence – the conceptual splitting up of life into fragments, dividing the great Undivided, and then believing in that division, taking that division as the reality. We have children now growing up feeling ugly, we have children desperate to be beautiful, trying to imitate the image of beauty we have spoon-fed to them. We cake ourselves in makeup, poke and tweak and mask ourselves, cover our beautiful imperfections, and often end up feeling less beautiful than ever, more alone than ever, more fake than ever, always striving for that elusive perfection, or at least that elusive "fitting in".

Screw brainwashing and the living of a second-hand life, forever seeking the approval or even acknowledgement of others! It's all beautiful, all of it! Or, at least, it's all a call to that underlying universal beauty that knows no opposite or bounds, the beauty of existence, of life itself, and everything, everything, is the invitation to this. The face of the homeless guy in the street, the stench of rotting things, the blood and the mucus and the sweat, it's all life, it's all holy, and though we might prefer some of this 'holiness' to holy itself away, still, despite our best efforts, it remains, to prod and poke and remind us to wake up to the vastness of things.

Every single one of your 'imperfections', every flaw, every crack and spot and line, every secretion, every smell that you try so hard to mask and hide, is a little invitation to remember your mortality, your underlying humility, your secret gratitude for things as they are, and your unfathomable and immense power as a unique expression of Life itself.

Be what you are. They have always said it, and it has always been true.

Don't let anyone tell you who or what is beautiful.

A LOVE THAT CANNOT FADE

If our love is dependent on looks, when looks fade, our love fades. If our love relies on feelings, when feelings weaken, our love is threatened. If our love is attached to stories, when stories cannot be remembered, our love is forgotten. If love clings to form, then when form dies, as it must, love dies too.

Is there a love that is not dependent on form or feeling? Is there a love with no conditions? Is there a love untouched by disease and death?

Of course there is. It is this loving presence that welcomes every thought, every sensation, every sound as its very own child, clinging to nothing, resisting nothing, saying, "I am what you are, so we cannot be divided."

And so, dear friend, I do not love you, I *am* you, beyond hope, beyond fear, beyond all conceptions of love and death...

VOICES OF ADDICTION AND FREEDOM

The voice of addiction: "I have forgotten who I am. I feel lack and incompleteness in the moment. I need X to give me back my fullness, my own presence, to remind me again of who I am. X will bring presence in the future. Presence is outside of me now. I am dependent on X. I need X."

The voice of freedom: "I know that nothing and nobody can take away this presence that I am. I feel the urge, the desire, the want for X. I acknowledge it, I even allow it – the sensations of the body, the pictures of the mind – but I know that X fundamentally cannot and will not give me anything that isn't already here. X will not bring presence, my true peace. Presence is Now. It is not outside of me, or contained in objects or people or substances – it is what I am in the deepest sense. The urge, the contraction, the sense of limitation, is not an enemy, but is actually reminding me of what I am – naturally vast and spacious, an unlimited, unchanging and ever-present room radically open to all of its changing contents. It is my inherent limitlessness that allows this sense of limitation. It is my natural relaxation that allow this sense of contraction. I am not dependent on X for present-moment peace. I do not need X. I am already whole, even without it. I am already whole, now."

Trying to allow this moment? Trying to escape this moment? Trying to surrender to it? *You're already too late!*

Present thoughts, sensations, sounds and feelings, are *already* here. The floodgates of this moment are already wide open, and cannot be closed. Present thoughts, sensations, sounds and feelings are already flooding in. In other words, "you" have already failed to block this moment out! There is simply nobody here in charge of the floodgates, nobody separate from life, nobody who can stem this wild flow of energy. What you are is helplessly, choicelessly, effortlessly, allowing this moment to be.

It is recognising the "already as it is" nature of experience that is the key to boundless freedom and unlimited creative expression, and even compassionate, intelligent action, however contradictory that sounds to the rational mind, which believes that change can only come from the story, that deep rest is merely stagnation and passivity, and that effortlessness can only come from effort.

Forget trying to allow or resist this moment, and forget trying to control life or to surrender that control, and recognise that on a deeper level, beyond understanding, this moment has already been completely allowed, and what you are feeling and sensing and smelling and tasting right now is only the result of total acceptance, prior to the upsurge of the image of "you" as the one who accepts or does not accept.

What you are, beyond the story, has already said *yes* to this moment in its totality.

STOP MAKING SENSE

Can it be okay, right now – and there is only now – for nothing to make sense anymore?

Sometimes it seems like everything in your world is in disarray. Everything that you thought was solid, certain, predictable, reliable, turns out to be paper-thin and subject to the laws of impermanence. The support and foundations of your life have crumbled away, or so it seems. There is a strange, empty feeling inside. The ground underneath you has dissolved, everything is spinning out of control, and you're living in a strange and even unfriendly universe. The past suddenly feels so unreal – like you've been living a lie all this time. Did it ever happen? And the future seems so uncertain and even scary – like it's made of glass and basically cannot be trusted. What is real? What can you hold on to?

Perhaps there has been no disaster, no great calamity, and the present whirlwind is only another giant invitation to be *here*. To live in this moment, the only moment there is. To actually turn towards this empty and ungrounded feeling, to deeply honour it, to allow it in. To say *yes* to life in all its myriad present appearances, *yes* to everything being uncertain right now, *yes* to everything spinning out of control, *yes* to none of it making sense, *yes* to your whole identity being a giant question mark. To take the focus off the story of time and space, and to bring loving focus back to the place you actually are, and will always be – here and now, your true home. To let go of the dreams, and sink into the sacred mystery of it all.

Perhaps then, in the midst of breakdown, the seeds of breakthrough can take root – planted with wisdom, watered with love, held in the warmth of your timeless presence.

THIS STRANGE PLACE

Can we meet beyond the story of us,
in the place beyond expectations,
and hold each other there?

Can we meet beyond the dream of tomorrow,
and rediscover what is here today,
so that today becomes tomorrow, effortlessly?

Haven't we always been meeting like this,
here at the edge of the world,
where everything is possible?

This strange place seems so familiar.

AWAKENING IS JUST THE BEGINNING

I have never met anyone who simply "woke up" one day, and never suffered again – however much we love to believe that story, about ourselves and others. I have never met anyone – teacher or student – who "discovered who they really were" and never, ever forgot it again, even in the midst of physical pain or the beautiful mess of intimate human relationship.

I spent years after my so-called 'awakening', meeting all of the unmet human conditioning, the childhood pain, the pain of all humanity, the unloved waves in the ocean of life, the feelings of failure and doubt and self-importance and arrogance and impotence and the need-to-be-perfect and the need-to-be-right, the forms that had been repressed or ignored or buried for at least a quarter of a century. Finally, in the absence of the urge to escape life, in the recognition that all was ultimately allowed in what I am, the human stuff was allowed to breathe and express and sing and dissolve in its own time. The personal purged itself in the impersonal fire of life, in the furnace of not-knowing, until it became absurd to even speak of the impersonal as distinct from the personal... or to even speak of 'my awakening' at all!

Liberation may be the end of a belief in a separate 'I', but really, my friends, this is just the beginning of the adventure, however much we want to think of it as some kind of 'end point'. It takes tremendous courage to drop the story of your own awakening, to be a child of life again, to admit that you really do not know a damn thing, and never did.

THIS MOMENT HAS NO OPPOSITE

This moment, whatever shape it takes, has no opposite. Investigate this very deeply, for this insight is the key to unimaginable peace:

Opposites only exist in thought. *Past/future, right/wrong, beautiful/ugly, enlightened/unenlightened, life/death,* all divisions made by thought. Can you find these divisions, these gaps, these clefts in reality, in direct experience?

Feeling has no opposite. Sensation has no opposite. Sound has no opposite. A bird singing in this moment has no opposite, only in the imagination ("bird singing" / "bird not singing"). That ineffable "Tweet! Tweet" has no opposite, though. This intense energy in the chest or stomach has no opposite. The raw feeling of life has no opposite, only in thought, only in images, only in the dream of time and space.

When you realise that in actuality this moment has no opposite, you stop trying to escape it. Since this moment has no opposite, it is not opposed by any other moment. It has no opposition, no enemy. It is a true original, unique in all of time and space, free to be itself, never at war.

Start an unexpected revolution. Realise deeply that this moment is all there is, and that it has no opposite, except as a picture in your head of how it 'should' be or 'could' have been. And realise that even that picture cannot oppose this moment. All is allowed.

FIRST CONTACT

Just one instant of naked contact
Changes everything

Just one instant of touching directly
your fear, anger, sadness, doubt, boredom, loneliness
Meeting the raw energy of life itself
Behind the labels and concepts
Prior to the words
Meeting 'what is' without expectation, without trying to escape,
without turning away, without protection
Forever changes your relationship to it

Now, you know each other directly, beyond theory
You have penetrated each other's defences
You have seen through the façade
You have truly made contact
And nothing will ever be the same

Now, however far you travel from each other
However much you try to push each other away
However desperately you try to forget each other
You will never truly forget
That you once met so deeply
That you have touched each other

And been touched in return
That you have held each other in the palms of your hands
And seen yourself reflected
And forgotten division
And the separation of things

Now, when fear appears again
Or when sadness returns in waves
Or when anger bursts forth from the creative void
Or a thought floats by
You will know
It is only a familiar friend
Come to visit
It is only the one you love
Brilliantly disguised

Just a moment of real contact
Is all it takes
And then there is no turning back

For you cannot truly forget
the one you love
your own child
your own flesh and blood

No matter how their appearance changes
No matter how far they roam

THE DARKNESS AND THE LIGHT

Humans have always thought in terms of abstract, conceptual opposites. *God and the devil, life and death, pleasure and pain, good and evil, yin and yang, duality and nonduality.*

Some people see life as a never-ending battle between darkness and light. Some hope that the light will win. Some take the side of the darkness. But is there really a war? Shadows only appear *because* there's a source of light. Shadows have no separate existence from light, no true power of their own. Shadows cannot truly oppose light, for without light they are nothing at all. They receive all their power from light. They are utterly dependent.

Light never needs to fear the shadows or long for their death or destruction. True light knows no opposite, no opposition, no mortal enemy. We pay so much attention to the darkness, to the 'negative' aspect, to the shadows, to what we see as the 'absence of light', not realising that the only reason we can recognise the darkness is because the light is still very much switched on. No light, no darkness. And we are that light, the timeless light of consciousness itself.

Don't fight the darkness. Use the appearance of darkness to remind you of the ever-present Light Source that you are. Don't oppose the shadows you see in the world, but know yourself as that timeless and limitless light of consciousness with ever more conviction, and you will come to realise that darkness was never 'against' you at all – it was only a reminder to never forget who you are, to see through the illusory division in yourself.

The war between darkness and light can never be won, for it never began.

MOMENT BY MOMENT

Suddenly, at home, at work or at play, a crisis happens. Something unexpectedly goes wrong. Something cherished is lost. Something familiar collapses. You feel misunderstood, abused, hurt, shocked, lost. Old, familiar friends now come to visit: That sinking feeling in the stomach. That shortness of breath. That tightness in the chest. That primal sense of disorientation. Who are you? What can be trusted? What will happen next? A dream of how life "was going to be" is dead and dying. An old identity is melting away. An old future has voided itself.

The invitation? Stay with this death. Breathe through it, breathe into it. Rest and stay present in the midst of the sudden movement. Ground yourself as the old ground falls away – it was never the true ground anyway. Know that only the false is crumbling, and the real cannot crumble. Remember, who you truly are cannot perish, only your plans can crumble and die. "My life" is always changing, that is its nature, so let the change be natural, and let the false crumble into the Life that you are. Let living truth reveal itself, moment by moment, without rewinding or fast-forwarding the movie. Lean into the seeming mess, relax into the present scene. See the aliveness and creativity in the cyclone – you are only witnessing the death of dreams. Who you are has known the passing of many storms. Know yourself as the deep and unshakeable calm at the storm's timeless eye. Crisis is not disaster, it is unexpected birth. This is your constant invitation.

OCTOBER

My sense of God is not a deity,

but a profound sense of wonder.

– Albert Einstein.

YOUR OTHER HALF

Stop looking for your 'other half', your 'soul mate', the one who will 'complete' you – they're already here. As awareness itself, your perfect partner is the world, exactly as it appears. The vast and spacious Room of You is already full to the brim with your beloved content: Thoughts, sensations, feelings, images, sounds, all dancing and singing within you in this moment. Emptiness and form – you were made for each other. This is the perfect union of that which was never divided.

Marry yourself, and let the wedding bells ring.

IT'S NEVER AS BAD AS YOU THINK

The worst thing you'll ever have to face in life is a thought, a sensation, an emotion, a sound, a smell, happening in *this* moment. However intense or unexpected that happening is, however much it destroys your dreams of what should have been, as consciousness itself, as the vast ocean in which every wave of thought, sensation and feeling is deeply allowed to arise and fall, there is always enough space in you, always enough room for life. You are limitless in your embrace.

Whatever is appearing – thought, sensation, feeling, image, sound – you have already said *yes* to it. That is why it is already here – because there was no separate, solid 'you' to block it out. The absence of a separate 'you' is the constant and timeless *yes* to life, however paradoxical that sounds.

In simple language, you will never have to face anything in present experience that you haven't already said *yes* to at the very depths of your being, however uncomfortable or intense or unexpected that wave of experience is. This knowing brings deep relaxation and trust in the face of what is to come. Then we can open to life rather than shutting ourselves off.

Knowing yourself as the boundless ocean of acceptance, as consciousness itself, fearlessly rest in your changeless and immutable nature.

Bring it on.

ON STRESS

Stress is the tension between 'what is' in this moment, and your image of how this moment should be. Stress is a narrow focus on a mental list of 'things to do', an imaginary burden of 'all the things that haven't been done yet'. Stress always involves future-thinking, premature fast-forwarding, a focus on *what's not here right now*.

When the focus shifts away from what is not present to what is present, from lack to what is fully here, from fast-forward to play, and instead of trying to complete a seemingly endless list of a thousand things, you simply do the next thing with your full attention and passion, lists get completed effortlessly, without stress, and even if they don't, creative solutions are found.

Relax. The only thing you ever have to do is to remember that you are not the doer.

A CONVERSATION WITH LONELINESS

"I feel lonely."

"Wonderful. An invitation to get intimate with loneliness."

"What do you mean?"

"Try this. Drop the word 'loneliness' for a moment. Feel the raw sensations directly in the body. Where do you feel them? Feel the prickles, the tickles, the vibrations…"

"In my stomach. Like a lonely, empty feeling…"

"Great. So now drop the words 'lonely' and 'empty'. Connect with what's actually here without those second-hand descriptions".

"Okay. It feels…………… alive. Tingly. Warm."

"Yes. Good. Stay with it."

"It feels soft. Tender. Vulnerable. It feels like… life."

"Good. Let's stay there awhile. Let's give these sensations the gift of kind attention, without trying to change or delete them. Allow all thoughts and images, all judgements and stories, to come and go as well, in your warm presence. Let them float like clouds in the sky. What else do you notice where you are? You can place your hand on the part of you that feels lonely, if you like…"

[*Places hands on stomach*]

"It's strange. As I give it attention, the tightness is easing. There's more room around the lonely feeling. Like it's held by something… something large, spacious…"

"Does that sense of spaciousness itself feel lonely?"

"No. It feels... intimate. Open. Alive. Not lonely. I feel like I can breathe..."

When we stop distracting ourselves, and courageously dive into the heart of any feeling, positive or negative, right or wrong, comfortable or uncomfortable, we rediscover the vast ocean of who we are. Every feeling is made of unspeakable intelligence, and every feeling contains a hidden message.

THE PLAN

With each of our breaths
We plug the gaping void.

We watch the eclipse of some other moon
In some other sky.

We don't know each other's names
Yet we stay close.

And against all advice to the contrary
We ride out without a plan.

We have nothing to hold onto anymore
Except this awesome sense
Of being alive.

Nothing to follow
Except this unmarked path of
never needing to know.

Nothing to speak of as 'real'
Except perhaps this love.
This unexpected grace.

You see my dear
Every journey has a beginning and an end.

Except this one.

DOORWAYS OF GRACE

The touch of a loved one's hand. The warmth of a fresh mug of tea. A drop of morning dew quietly falling down a blade of grass, nearly unnoticed. These ordinary moments, given without asking.

And yet, in truth, these are not 'ordinary moments' at all. These are only doorways of grace, gateless gates of morning dew and birdsong and tossed apple cores, portals into an unknown world much like our own, witnessed without a witness, prior to the upsurge of thought.

"Enter here," they whisper in unison, "and lose your cleverness..."

YOUR THRILLING INCONSISTENCY

You can tell all kinds of stories about yourself. "I am good". "I am bad". "I am kind". "I am perfect". "I am enlightened". "I am unworthy". "I am a failure". "I am beautiful". "I am ugly". And so on.

But these are all mental *conclusions* about something that is not a single 'thing' at all – something alive and always moving and forever renewing itself, something that is never, ever a conclusion. You are a vast ocean, a wild fire, dynamic and untameable and inconsistent, not anything static or fixed in time or space. Why come to conclusions about yourself at all? Any conclusion cannot be what you really are, for you are beyond all conclusions, even that one, and yet there is enough space in you for all conclusions.

But life itself is not a conclusion – conclusions are only there to be swept away and burnt up in the fire of living. Why limit yourself to a concept? Why fix yourself in time and space? Be your thrilling inconsistent 'self' – not a 'self' limited to a word, concept, idea or image, or even limited in time itself, but the vast indefinable Self of the ocean, wildly open and deeply accepting of all its beloved waves yet defined by none of them, limited to none of them.

BEYOND UP AND DOWN

It's exhausting, trying or pretending to be 'up' all the time. What a relief it is, to embrace 'down' too, and to see 'up' and 'down' as part of the great and perfect balance of life. And to know ourselves beyond both, as the vast open space that embraces these slings and arrows, these tribulations and triumphs of existence, and is trapped within neither. Ups and downs, highs and lows, tragedies and comedies, bliss and boredom and buses running late, birth and burials – the many faces of the One, moment to moment, shining brilliantly.

I was speaking to a young man who was dealing with severe anxiety. None of the 'cures for anxiety' he had been offered had worked for him. I invited him to stop trying to fix his anxiety, just for a moment. I invited him to stop imagining a future free from anxiety, or filled with anxiety, and to meet what was actually here, right now, in this present scene. I invited him to drop the label 'anxiety', to let go of that word he had learned, to come out of his story of past and future and look at his present experience with fresh eyes and without history. What thoughts and sensations were appearing presently?

Lots of thoughts buzzing around, he said. Lots of mental activity. What did he feel in his body? I invited him to contact the body directly. Intense fluttery sensations in the stomach and chest. I asked him if, just for a moment, he could allow all that activity – thoughts and sensations – to be there, something he had never tried before, because he had been too busy fighting his 'anxiety'; a fight which, of course, had actually increased his anxiety! He had been making 'anxiety' his enemy, rejecting it, trying to delete it, without getting to know it intimately first! Instead of fighting the sensations in the stomach, could he drop all labels, all judgements, all descriptions, and recognise himself as the vast open space in which these sensations were allowed to come and go? Could he be friendly to these sensations, just for a moment? Could kindness be the way?

He started to feel some space around what he had previously been calling 'anxiety'. He was aware of the anxiety, he was conscious of it, so it couldn't truly define who he was. He was no longer trapped in the feelings. He was bigger than the feelings. He could hold his anxiety, surround it, embrace it. And the thoughts and judgements too, he was bigger than those. He was not trapped inside them – he was the space for them. They didn't define him.

He had been able to turn towards his anxiety, and had used it as a wake-up call, to help him remember his true vastness. He had discovered that, in truth, there was no 'anxious person' – the anxiety could not define or limit the vastness of who he was – there were simply thoughts and sensations that had been labelled as 'anxiety' and then rejected. He was not a victim of anxiety – he was now its loving parent, able to hold it as it was born, expressed itself, and died. His anxiety didn't need to be 'cured' – it needed to be met, touched, held, in the present moment. It didn't need to be deleted, it needed to be understood. It didn't want to destroy him, it wanted to wake him up. It wasn't a mistake that he had felt anxious.

Healing in the midst of anxiety – the last place you'd ever think to look!

A DONE DEAL

How can you allow this moment? How can you accept it? Wouldn't you have to be separate from it, to accept it? How can you allow the air, the rain, the grass as it grows? How can you allow the planets to spin in their orbits? How can you allow the breath in your lungs? Isn't all of this already allowed? Isn't life already exactly as it is right now? How can you allow or disallow what is already here? Isn't it already too late to accept or reject this moment? How can you surrender to something you were never separate from in the first place? Hasn't The Deepest Acceptance already happened?

ON LONELINESS

Loneliness is the memory or imagination of past connection and companionship, a painful comparison between 'what is now' and 'what was then'. It is an impossible homesickness, a longing to return Home, where Home is 'not here anymore', somewhere seemingly 'far away' from presence.

Cease to focus on what is 'missing' – the absent presence of 'another' – and simply remember what is, and was, never missing – your own presence, timeless and full, your true Home – and you will never feel lonely again, since your presence *is* their presence.

Loneliness will always arise, when it needs to, to remind you that you've forgotten to remember who you are. A brand new invitation every time.

How can you be lonely when the entire universe purrs at your feet?

THE LESSONS OF THE DYING

When we die, we do not become infinite. We were always infinite, so we cannot die.

Sitting with the dying is such a privilege. In the absence of a tomorrow, in the face of absolute uncertainty and ungroundedness in terms of the story, total intimacy is all that is left, total presence, profound hereness. Every moment is rendered absolutely sacred – as it always was. Every breath is precious. Every word is there to be deeply heard and savoured, every touch reverberates throughout the ages, every look, every glance, all that is said and unsaid, all that is remembered and all that is lost to time, all is held in the vast embrace of Now, the only place we truly meet, the only place we have ever met. What happens 'next' is secondary in the face of this fire-like intimacy, untouched by death and dying and the dreams of tomorrow.

You cannot leave me, for we are each other, and where would we go? Come into my heart, where you always were, and I will take you with me.

THE FURNACE OF THE BELOVED

It emerges from the Womb with you.
It sees the world for the first time.
It has no other eyes but these.

The world is its furnace, its playground of fire.

It grows with you. Changes. Hurts. Rejoices.
It learns exactly what you learn.
All the conditioning in the world cannot condition it away.

It goes through each rite of passage.
First kiss. Wedding day. Graduation.
It feels everything as intensely as you do.

And on your retirement day, it retires with you.
And when your loved ones die, it mourns with you.
It misses them too.

Its tears only dry when yours do.

It falls asleep with you every night.
It holds you as you go for chemo.
It forgets its medication in perfect synchronicity.
It does not know good and bad.

It gives you just enough energy to stand where you stand.
To sit where you sit. To lie where you lie.
It does not know failure or success.

It soils itself if it has to.

And even when the pain becomes unbearable,
It whispers "I am still here".
"I take unexpected forms".

Its heart stops when yours does.
It takes its last breath with you.
Not even in these moments can it leave.
Not even in these moments.

It does not know coming and going.

You may cry out, "Where are You?"
"Why have You forsaken me?"
But at no point does this question go unanswered.

For your cry is its cry,
Your question is its question.
It is forever calling Itself home in this way,
Never, ever needing an answer.

Listen, and you can hear it calling, always.

Listen – it is there even when you cannot hear it call.
For it hears exactly what you hear.
No more and no less.

We all burn in its fire.
Our bones melt in its loving embrace.

Do not fear the furnace of the Beloved.
It has already taken you.

NOVEMBER

The deeper that sorrow carves into your being,

the more joy you can contain.

– Kahlil Gibran

Who is willing to stare life in the face?

Who is willing to abandon second-hand concepts about second-hand revelations, forge their own path, and neither cling to the paths of others nor reject a single one of them?

Who is willing to never settle for easy answers, no matter how comforting those answers may sound in the midst of our pain?

Who is willing to let go of those spiritual clichés – "there is no me", "free will is an illusion", "everything is a concept" – which once sounded so exciting and new and even controversial, but now just feel stale, overused, and a little sad?

Who is willing to throw away their books, cease quoting endlessly from their favourite perceived authorities, find their own language and unique voice, and dive into a first-hand life that nobody else has ever lived or could live?

Who is willing to sacrifice their certainty, their credibility, their intellectual prowess and so-called 'spiritual success' for one shot at a life fully experienced?

Who is willing to consider that this day may be their final day to experience anything at all?

Who is ready to risk everything for the rapture of uncertainty, doubt, shattered dreams, mystery, and blood pumping through enlivened veins?

Who will join me in this creative fire?

THE MIRACLE

There is no such thing as a miracle from God when you realise that everything in present experience is a miracle from God, every taste, every sound, every smell, each vibrantly alive feeling surging out of the vastness, and so the words 'miracle' and 'God' are unnecessary, and it is enough to simply be alive, here and now, breathing in and out, feeling the expansion and contraction of the chest, savouring the richness and immediacy of the moment, God or no God, miracle or otherwise...

THE ENLIGHTENMENT GAMES

So many spiritual teachers. So many teachings. So many words. So many flavours. Who to believe?

Some speak of awakening as an event. It happens one day, and you're never the same again.

Some speak of awakening as a process. Events, states and experiences come and go, but the ever-deepening journey of awakening never ends.

Some say there is nobody here, no person, no self, no entity that could experience an event, or go on any kind of journey, and there's no point talking about it anyway, and yet they keep talking about it.

Some stay silent. Some claim to be right, to have the truth, to know exactly what awakening is and what it is not. Some want you to join their 'awakening club', to be on their side. Some see awakening as a kind of competition, race or game. Some make fun of other teachings and teachers who don't tow the party line.

All of this is part of the great play of life. We rest as the witness of the play, and delight in the play's myriad colours.

A PASSIONATE PARADOX

The essential understanding at the heart of all the world's religious and spiritual traditions: We are all absolutely, radically One, *and* we are all totally unique expressions *of* that One.

In our essence we are all the same ocean – consciousness itself – but each of us is a totally unique and never-to-be-repeated wave of that ocean, an original expression of this unspeakable life force.

We are individuals but indivisible, we are one but we are not the same, and to fall too deeply into either polarity of that universal balance leads to suffering, either in the form of depression and neurosis (getting bogged down in our personal story with all its fears, and exhausting ourselves with our never-ending quest to improve and perfect and save ourselves in the future) or, on the other side, in the form of spiritual bypassing and premature transcendence (detaching from the body, repressing or even denying our humanness, losing our humour and humility, pretending to be 'above' mortal concerns, floating away into blissfully painful ungrounded transcendent states and even psychosis, and losing our lifeblood, that essential love and compassion for ourselves and all humanity).

To live passionately with the paradox of the absolute and the relative, of nothing and everything, of personal and impersonal, of being the ocean and, at exactly the same time, being a unique and never-to-be-repeated wave of that ocean, to see the mystery and even the joke and the joy in this paradox, to dance with it without trying to 'solve' it or come to mental conclusions about it, is the beating heart of this creative adventure that we call life.

The Absolute is not absolute, it relativises itself absolutely, and that is love.

DREAMS

To dream, yes, to dream! And yet, to hold those dreams in a sweet, feather-light embrace, knowing they are loved even when they cannot sustain themselves, even when they crumble and turn to dust.

To dream, yes, to dream! But to recognise yourself as the silent, restful background of dreams and their failure, to know yourself as the awakeness that loves to dream even though it is always awake.

So dream, hope, change and seek change, fight for those who do not have a voice! And yet know that you are Home, always, and that even in the midst of the rubble of dashed hopes and plans and failed dreams, in the lostness you have always feared, in the absence of a future, I will call your name, I will find you in the darkness, I will take your hand, I will show you a love the likes of which you never could have dreamed.

Friend, you are doing better than you could ever imagine.

MOVING, UNMOVING

The sun rises and sets in the sky that it never calls 'sky'. What never changes?

The universe expands and contracts and expands again. What never changes?

Organisms are born and soon pass away into deep rest. What never changes?

The breath goes in and out, in and out. What never changes?

Seasons transform in the blink of an eye. What never changes?

You taste it all: Laughter and tears, bliss and boredom, the slings and arrows of existence. What never changes?

What never changes is the constancy of change. Change is absolutely trustworthy!

And in the midst of inevitable change, what never changes? That which recognises change as change. That which sees change and says 'change'. That which sees change doesn't change with change, otherwise there could be no recognition of change. The recognition, because of the contrast, is an expression of infinite intelligence.

You are present, changeless and unmoving, ageless, never changing with change but standing in fascination and awe and wonder at the ever-changing display of life itself. You naturally embrace change but never yourself change. This is why, deep down, you have always felt like you haven't aged, even though your body has aged. Change is never your enemy but your most loyal ally and partner. It is the reason manifestation can be experienced at all.

Thoughts, sensations, feelings. Galaxies moving in the morning darkness, planets whirling around their familiar orbits, the birds chirping spontaneous songs of joy in springtime, your grandfather's ashes scattered by the river in which he splashed gleefully as a child, never knowing what was to come. All of this spilled out of your ancient heart. You couldn't withhold all of that creativity.

THE FORM AND THE EMPTINESS

Scientists now know what mystics realised long ago: Energy is matter, matter is energy, and all is One, and One is for All, not merely a select or lucky few. The material is spiritual; there is no division.

Abstract human thought, in its quest for fixed and unchanging meaning in a groundless universe, divided an indivisible reality into isolated fragments, objects, things, which it then took to be the true reality. Out of the vast and incomprehensible ocean of Being, we said 'I' and 'world', dividing ourselves out as a separate entity, plunging ourselves into a lifelong search for the Home-world we never left. We worshipped false idols, the idols of thought, living as a 'self' in a separate 'world', forgetful of our true nature as life itself, longing for rest.

But no matter. For matter is energy, and energy is matter, and in this moment, it really doesn't matter that we ever dreamed of leaving Home. *Wake up, Dorothy.* For we are still Here, and it is still Now, and Oneness never changes in the midst of unending change. Energy cannot be created or destroyed, and so all is well, child, all is well.

That look in your father's eyes as he passes into infinity says it all. Love can only recycle itself.

A trillion light-years away, comets shoot through the darkness in silence.

SEASONS OF AWAKENING

Spiritual awakening is not a linear path towards some fixed goal, nor is it the total absence of a path, for who could deny the appearance of change, evolution and deepening insight?

It is a circular path, a path of poetry and song, always returning to where it began, always pointing us back to where we already are. Its origin is its destination, and its destination its origin, just as spring gives way to summer, then autumn and winter, but always returns to spring, the same spring, the same freshness, essentially unchanged by the passing of a year, but still, never the same at all.

Awakening is neither a path nor pathless, it is like the seasons, ever changing and yet always the same, timelessly stable yet radically open to impermanence, naked in the face of the bitter-sweet disappearance of things.

REST

A sip of tea. The gentle, last touch of a loved one's hand. A flurry of tingling sensation surging through the body. A stranger turning into a long-lost friend overnight. The incessant beeping of an IV machine. The sting of a needle that won't enter its vein. The bittersweet chirp of a morning bird. An afternoon breeze, gentle on your cheek. This, the first and last day of your life. Ecstasy, and laundry. Love, and pain. This stunning ordinariness, rich with miracle, overflowing with grace beyond our conception of it. The completion of life within its very appearance. So rest, weary seeker. Rest in this. Always.

THE IRRESISTABLE MOMENT

Admit it. You've already completely failed to resist this moment. This moment is totally irresistible to you! These thoughts, sensations, feelings, sounds, are already here. They are already freely arising and dissolving in what you are. Nothing has been able to block them out. There is simply no 'you' getting in the way of life. No boundaries. No barriers. The floodgates are already open, and life is pouring in. Utter nakedness.

Raise the white flag, soldier!

The healthiest relationships are not necessarily the ones that look 'happiest' to the naked eye. They aren't necessarily the ones where two people are always seen holding hands, giggling, dancing and singing with the butterflies, where nothing ever 'goes wrong' and life is always perfect. External perfection can easily mask internal devastation, disconnection and a quiet, unspoken desperation to be free, or at least alone.

The healthiest relationships are the honest ones, the ones that might not always look 'happy' or 'carefree' from the outside. The ones that might not fit society's image of what a relationship 'should' or 'must' look or feel like. Where two people tell the truth about today, and continually let go of all their preconceived ideas about each other. Where the relationship is forever renewed in the furnace of honesty. Where there may be ruptures, misunderstandings, even intense feelings of doubt and disconnection, but there is a mutual willingness to face this seeming mess head-on! To look – with open eyes – at the present rupture, and not turn away or cling to the past. To sit together in the midst of mutual shattered dreams and expectations, and work to find a place of reconnection, here, now, today. Where relationship is seen as the ultimate yoga – an ongoing and deepening adventure and rediscovery of each other, a constant meeting, not a future destination, fixed conclusion, point of arrival, or a convenient story to tell others during polite conversation.

As Eckhart Tolle reminds us, relationships aren't here to make us happy (for true happiness lies within) – they're here to make us profoundly conscious.

ALONE IN THE RAIN

Walking alone in the rain, bathed in consciousness, soaked in consciousness, consciousness as the raindrops, as the body they fall
upon, as the splish-splash on the sidewalk, as the incomprehensible intelligence that opens the umbrella exactly on cue, making
a mockery of the concept of the existence or non-existence of a
separate 'I'. And the raindrops whisper that the enlightenment
we seek is not cold detachment, or unfeeling world-denial, or
transcendence of the so-called 'material' world–no, it's this
unspeakable intimacy with the appearance of form, with this
ever-changing watercolour scenery of life, its colours forever
running into the gutters of emptiness. "Love us", the raindrops
whisper. "That's all".

And I smile to myself at the seriousness and the mad, cosmic
innocence of the spiritual search, the search for something more
than *this*. For who could want or seek anything more than what
is already given? Still, the raindrops keep falling, and I walk on,
embraced by a love with no name.

DECEMBER

It not a cry that you hear at night,

It's not somebody who's seen the light,

It's a cold and it's a broken Hallelujah.

– Leonard Cohen, *Hallelujah*

THE VAULT

There is a locked vault containing everything you've ever longed for – all the riches of the universe.

You spend your life trying to open the vault – through struggling, striving, meditating, transcending, guru-worshipping, believing, rejecting, accepting, praying, self-inquiring, yoga-ing, and so on and so forth. Finally, exhausted, you give up trying to open the vault... and that's when the vault opens by itself. It was never locked in the first place.

What's inside the vault? *This moment, exactly as it is.*

You always knew.

THE DEATH OF TOMORROW

While working as a home carer, one morning I found myself washing faeces off a man's giant, swollen testicles. He was dying of a cancer which had spread throughout his testicles and prostate, and in the night he had defecated and rolled all around in the mess. We laughed a lot together and we chatted about football and the latest news stories as I cleaned him up. He could barely move, he was so sore and swollen everywhere. He was myself in disguise.

He had a few weeks to live, but he was so alive, so in the here-and-now, without a trace of self-pity. There was no loss of dignity there – there was just what was happening in the moment. He had somehow found a way to deeply accept his circumstances, even though his life had not turned out the way he had dreamed when he was younger and he had time to dream. It took over two hours to get him ready for his day, to hoist him out of his dirty bed, to get him washed and dressed and into his favourite chair. He didn't live for long after that. But I will always remember him.

Even when tomorrow never comes, we are nothing less than divine.

UNFORGETTABLE

Love, knowing that the one you love may not be here tomorrow, knowing that today may be your last day to truly meet, knowing that you cannot know how the story ends. For what is left in this life when you have nothing to lose?

Care, care deeply, care until it hurts, care in spite of what people say, care in spite of ridicule and rejection and misunderstandings, care so much that you no longer care what happens to you.

Sink, sink willingly, into the bitter-sweet mystery of love, never knowing what love is and loving anyway, like a fool, like a fascinated child, like a madman, like one who has forgotten how to be cynical, or how to be right.

Love until your voice trembles, and your heart pounds, and your legs shake, and your philosophies crumble to dust, and your cleverness bows its head in shame and in reverence.

And you will be taken to the darkest places, and your heart will be set on fire by the ones to whom you were never able to open your heart, and you will be reminded of what you have always, secretly, known:

In time, you will forget everything, except how to die, and how to love.

A MEDITATION BELL

So much of our suffering comes down to fear of loss of control, a resistance to chaos, a frantic search for some kind of order in the midst of a passing storm.

But chaos can actually be a great healer. Sometimes the storm needs to blow, the tempest needs to rage. Sometimes strong energies need to move and be felt fully. Sometimes feelings need to become more intense before they can dissipate. Sometimes hearts need to break wide open. Sometimes archaic dreams and plans need to fall away to make way for the new and the unexpected. Sometimes relationships need to change form, an old sense of self needs to die, familiar structures need to crumble, even though the mind wants them to stay the same.

We are plunged into the chaos and disorder of not knowing who or what or why-the-hell we are anymore, desperately seeking something to cling to – we feel homeless and we seek home. But the storm contains a powerful invitation to presence, your true home beyond your worldly home. The chaos invites us to remember the true source of unshakeable power and order – ourselves.

DO NOT SEEK OUTSIDE OF YOURSELF FOR HAPPINESS, the storm bellows. You will suffer until you realise this, and then you will suffer every time you forget it, and so suffering is not an enemy but a meditation bell in a storm, part of life's ingenious invitation.

MEET A FEELING WITHOUT HISTORY

Next time a wave of sadness, or anger, or doubt, or fear, or some kind of nameless despair, appears in the present moment, ask yourself: *Can this movement of life simply be allowed right now?* Don't try to find its cause or its solution; don't try to analyse it or work out the answers right now. The answers may come in time. The solutions may appear. But right now is the invitation to know yourself in the midst of the mess as the wide open space for all that appears, the capacity for it, the home for it, not its victim or slave. Let all feelings be embraced in the loving arms of your presence, just for a moment. Even if thought tries to push 'what is' away, or judge it, or spins off into planning and regret, notice that even thought-movements are allowed in the spacious awareness that you are. Notice how there is always enough space here, even for feelings of limitation and lack.

Nothing can distract you from meditation, when everything becomes part of meditation. This is meditation without a path, without a goal, without a script. It is meeting everything within you as a good friend.

A HOME FOR THOUGHTS

Natural peace and contentment means knowing yourself as the wide open space in which thoughts come and go, rather than the separate "thinker" or "controller" of those thoughts. You don't have thoughts – you naturally provide the space, the home, the resting place, for them. Thoughts are your children, too, and they deserve a home.

Since you can notice thoughts, be aware of them, recognise them as thoughts, it's clear that thoughts cannot define, limit or contain you. If they could, you'd never be able to say "that's a thought".

Just behind, around the edges, and infusing every thought, the unspeakable vastness of you.

NEVER TURN AWAY

And so we make this radical commitment to never turn away. Grounded in an unshakeable knowing – that has nothing to do with the mind's limited idea of certainty – that every sensation, every sound, every smell, every thought, every image, every possible feeling, is already deeply allowed to move and express in us, and recognising ourselves as the warm oceanic embrace of these beloved children, we simply cease to doubt our boundless ability to face life.

And if doubt does appear, and if a sense of 'my inability to face life' is what we're facing right now, we simply notice that even these waves are allowed in – already, timelessly allowed in the boundless capacity that we are.

And what are we left with? Only unspeakable gratitude for the tiniest and most 'insignificant' of things. A breath. The taste of an orange. This untameable and unnameable aliveness we call the body. The wild mystery of the eyes. Live, dear friend, live this day, this ordinary day, this sacred day, this one and only day, knowing that in some incomprehensible way it has already fulfilled your heart's true desire.

The heart shatters into a million pieces in ecstasy, because finally you have remembered to never abandon yourself.

SPLISH SPLASH

The rain does not fall all at once. It hits the ground, not as some entity called 'rain', but drop by drop, moment by precious moment, impersonal and free. 'Rain' is only a metaphor. *Splish splash.*

Thought remembers the last drop, and anticipates the next drop. This is how suffering is created.

Remembering the last drop, and the many drops before that, adds the heaviness of "my painful and burdensome past" to the present drop.

Remembering yesterday's absence of rain, yesterday's dryness, even yesterday's blissful sunshine, adds the pain of longing and regret to the present drop.

Dreaming of the next drop, and the many drops to come, projecting a future downpour, adds the anxiety of "my painful and heavy future" to the present drop.

But in actuality, without history, and without dreams of the future, there is only the present drop, this fresh new drop. And whether the present pain-drop is huge and intense, or soft and gentle, it is always happening Now, and we are always spared from the ravages of time.

The rain does not fall all at once. *Splish splash.*

ASCENSION

Awakening. Enlightenment. Higher and higher levels of consciousness. Seeking the light. Becoming the light. Being the light.
Going beyond the light. Receiving transmission. Giving trans-
mission. Sitting at the feet of the guru. Excitement. *The guru
must know.* Burning incense. Reading spiritual books. Chanting.
Meditating. Doing yoga. Liberating the inner child. *Getting there,
getting there.* Discovering the true self. Transcending the ego.
Going beyond mind. Ascending. Descending. Ascending again.
Opening chakras. Attaining unimaginable powers. Miracles.
Inexplicable feats. Mysterious happenings. Insight upon insight.
Being human. Non-human. Trans-human. Meta-human. Going
beyond duality. Going beyond going beyond duality. Going
beyond "going beyond going beyond". Who goes beyond? Seeing
the non-existence of the 'I'. The source of Self. Who sees? Who
asks?

Stop, friend. Breathe.

Your elderly father's hand brushes against yours as you walk
together through the park. Never to be repeated, a moment.

Contact. An insurrection.

Be here, it whispers. *You get this only once. Be here.*

A PRAYER FOR THE DYING

Life,

Let them struggle to understand until there is only confusion,
and in the centre of that confusion show them their inherent
clarity.

Make them courageous by taking away all of their hope,
and let them weep until their stomachs hurt,
until their tears melt into laughter.

Love them by destroying them.

And when they are more alone than ever,
show them an intimacy they cannot imagine.

Make them suffer until they are exhausted from fighting You,
make their pain great enough so that all their concepts turn to
dust and ash.

Let them never know what they are looking for,
but make them keep looking anyway,
as if their lives depended on it.

Give them time to read their books and listen to their teachers,
give them time to build up mountains of knowledge,

give them certainty and pride and a sense of security.

And then let their books rot,
and turn their teachers into hypocrites,
and make them doubt and forget everything they've learned.

Everything.

And make them stand alone, facing You,
naked and without protection,
and let them tremble,
let them wet themselves with fear,
let all masks and pretensions fall away.

And then let them into the great secret,
that they are loved beyond words,
in their nakedness, in their failure, in their brokenness,
in everything they were running away from.

That they are you.
That your face is their face.

That nothing ever happened at all.

NOTHING TO LOSE

Do it–or let it be done–the thing for which your heart has always been waiting.

What is the risk? Losing everything? Then lose everything. The experience of failure? Then experience failure, taste it, find a new kind of success within it. Rejection? Then open up to the glory of rejection, open your heart wide to the ones who reject you, see their pain and forgive them for it. Ridicule? Then fall in love with those voices of ridicule, seeing them as your beloved new-borns, your own voices in need of kind attention.

Life is too precious to waste, and too immediate to postpone, and the 'worst' that could happen is a broken body or a shattered image, neither of which are really who you are. Nothing to lose, except perhaps your imaginary pride, your frightened ego which secretly longs to burn in the furnace of living anyway...

RUBY SLIPPERS

There are no ordinary moments. We have always known this, deep down, for we were young once, and we still are. We just pretended to be 'grown ups', that's all. Life is still the cosmic adventure it always was. You are perfect exactly as you are.

It is not the 'me' that awakens. Awakening cannot enter the story, for it is beyond time and space and cannot be some kind of conclusion for a 'person'. The awakening is from the mirage of 'me', with its myriad projects, its plans, its conclusions, its incessant seeking for more, and its never-ending holding up of the image, including the image of itself as some kind of Wizard of Oz, some superhuman, Christ-like figure, some hyper-awakened being sent down from heaven to save the mortals.

For some, awakening is sudden. For many, it is gradual, over a lifetime. For all, it is timeless, and for all, the destination is the same – Kansas, Source, Presence, Home – and the destination is the origin, and it all points to this moment exactly as it is, right now. Stunningly ordinary, yet as vast as the universe, as rich and as full as the Ganges at sunrise, as precious as that look in your child's eyes, so easily forgotten, so easily remembered.

There's no place like Home – the present moment. The Emerald City, however colourful and exciting, doesn't even come close to the intimacy and majesty of a single instant of being alive. Only empty magpie-promises live in that shining city of light and darkness, and the *following, following, following, following, following* of false prophets living and dying for profit.

There's no place like Home. Click your heels together three times and say it. Nothing to lose.

GRATITUDE

Despite the sorrow and the despair, despite the times when I thought I'd never make it, despite the days when the mind seemed like a torture chamber and the body a prison, despite the years of pain and profound alienation from my true nature, it has been a blessed life, a life of unspeakable riches, and I wouldn't have wanted it any other way, and it couldn't have been any other way.

And if it all ends tomorrow, if the curtain falls, I will be reduced to a word, there will be only a single word left, and that word will be the word that started it all, and that word will be Gratitude.

Thank you. For everything – the light and the darkness, the gain and the loss, the success and the failure, the pleasure and the pain, the joy and the sorrow, and for the unspeakable awareness in which it all came and went like birdsong.

ACKNOWLEDGEMENTS

With thanks to Nic Higham (www.nichigham.com) for your generous help with the text and cover design, and Matt Licata for your endless encouragement and beautiful foreword. Mum, thanks for the feedback and the friendship, and for the birth. Julian and Catherine, it's good to be home. Robin, Barry, Sid, John, Yoko, Menno, Jeannine and Mike, gratitude for your friendship and encouragement over the years. And to all you other shining stars, countless in number, who made everything possible, thank you from the bottom of my heart.

Index of First Lines

CPSIA information can be obtained at www.ICGtesting.com
Printed in the USA
BVOW04s1412061213

338320BV00002B/49/P

9 781908 664396